THE COLLECTED WORKS OF

ERIC VOEGELIN

VOLUME 18

ORDER AND HISTORY

VOLUME V

IN SEARCH OF ORDER

ORDER AND HISTORY

The Editorial Board offers grateful acknowledgment to the Earhart
Foundation, Liberty Fund, Inc., Robert J. Cihak, M.D.,
and John C. Jacobs Jr. for support provided at various stages in the
preparation of this book for publication. A special thanks for
support goes to the Charlotte and Walter Kohler Charitable Trust.

The University of Missouri Press offers its grateful acknowledgment for a
generous contribution from the Eric Voegelin Institute.

THE COLLECTED WORKS OF

ERIC VOEGELIN

VOLUME 18

ORDER AND HISTORY

VOLUME V

IN SEARCH OF ORDER

EDITED WITH AN INTRODUCTION BY
ELLIS SANDOZ

UNIVERSITY OF MISSOURI PRESS
COLUMBIA AND LONDON

Library of Congress Cataloging-in-Publication Data

Voegelin, Eric, 1901
    Order and history.
        p.   cm.—(The collected works of Eric Voegelin ; v. 18)
    Originally published: Baton Rouge : Louisiana State University Press, 1956–
1987. With new introd.
    Includes bibliographical references and index.
    Contents: — v. 5. In search of order / edited with an introduction by Ellis Sandoz.
    ISBN 0-8262-1261-1 (v. 5 : alk. paper)
    1. Civilization—Philosophy.   2. Order (Philosophy)   I. Sandoz, Ellis, 1931-   .
II. Title.
    CB19.V58   2000
    901—dc21   99-053537

⊗™ This paper meets the requirements of the American National Standard
    for Permanence of Paper for Printed Library Materials, Z39.48, 1984.

Designer: Albert Crochet
Typesetter: Bookcomp, Inc.
Printer and binder: Thomson-Shore, Inc.
Typeface: Trump Mediaeval

Contents

IN SEARCH OF ORDER

Editor's Introduction

No full-scale introduction by the editor is needed for this slender volume. The one I wrote twelve years ago for the original edition remains serviceable enough today, and Jürgen Gebhardt's valuable epilogue also can be consulted. Yet one or two points should be emphasized and some notice be taken of the valuable literature inspired by this book as the culmination of *Order and History* (1956–1987).

First, this last book effects Voegelin's definitive theoretical break with Enlightenment rationalism as the form of modern philosophy and its replacement by meditative rationality or *noesis*, thereby reviving a mode of inquiry that goes back to Saint Augustine's *Confessions* and to Plato's dialogues. The book itself is a persuasive analysis of meditative analysis as the substantial form of philosophizing requisite, if the exploration of the heights and depths of reality is to be conducted in openness to truth and not be vitiated by reductionist deformations of one kind or another. Such meditative analysis, in turn, constitutes the core of the renewed science of human affairs Voegelin struggled to establish and to elucidate in his work of a lifetime. On the one hand, it is an act of resistance against the truncated and mendacious accounts of reality rife in our ideological age, with disastrous consequences for personal and political order. On the other hand, it is an enterprise in which the author was self-consciously and explicitly engaged at least from the time of the unpublished *"Herrschaftslehre"* (ca. 1930) onward, most powerfully so in the late works. Far from being something new in this little book, the structuring of inquiry on the model of *fides quaerens intellectum* is taken to be emblematic of philosophy itself from its pre-Socratic origins—the love of wisdom of a questing soul responsive to the divine appeal that rises in wonder toward more luminous participation in eminent reality. Voegelin's work corrects a derailment of philosophy he discovered occurring already in the generation after Aristotle, one that includes the Christian denaturing of *Nous* as "natural reason" (58).

Second, the mode of inquiry thus characterized, and pursued by a person amenable to the designation "mystic philosopher," understands the activity and life it unfolds as consistent with common sense and as representative of what it means to be a human being. Voegelin steadily held that all good philosophy is rooted in common sense and that the primary dimension of noetic reason (*nous*) is tension toward the divine ground of being. Thus, as readily as we acknowledge that this book can and should be placed side by side with the great meditative classics of history, we acknowledge in the next breath that the common humanity of all men finds its vital center and its deepest satisfactions in the spiritual life to which all are called, however imperfect each person's response to the divine appeal may in fact be. The intricacies of the meditation before us all dissolve into the reflective understanding of ordinary intelligence and common experience. Just don't stop thinking, Voegelin sometimes suggested. Or, to remember another exhortation he favored, a book that is not over your head is not worth reading. And he admired T. S. Eliot's sentiment that the only method in philosophical matters is to be very intelligent. Presumably even being intelligent does not place mystic philosophy beyond the sphere of the brotherhood of man under God. Eliot's requirement may in fact suggest that some of those who most loudly profess bafflement and incomprehension at Voegelin's texts provide evidence of the inroads of corruption, incapacity, and deculturation in supposedly educated readers, mostly a reflection of their own shortcomings.

For the considerable literature that has appeared on the central aspects of Voegelin's thought the great bibliography compiled by Geoffrey L. Price should be consulted, "Eric Voegelin Classified Bibliography," *Bulletin of the John Rylands University Library of Manchester* 76, no. 2 (summer 1994); this is updated in Stephen A. McKnight and Geoffrey L. Price, eds., *International and Interdisciplinary Perspectives on Eric Voegelin* (Columbia: University of Missouri Press, 1997), 189–214, which also contains several valuable essays. Of importance for themes of this book I should mention: Michael P. Morrissey, *Consciousness and Transcendence:*

The Theology of Eric Voegelin (Notre Dame: University of Notre Dame Press, 1994), esp. chaps. 4 and 6; Glenn Hughes, ed., *The Politics of Soul: Eric Voegelin on Religious Experience* (Lanham: Rowman & Littlefield, 1999); Glenn Hughes, *Mystery and Myth in the Philosophy of Eric Voegelin* (Columbia: University of Missouri Press, 1993); Kenneth Keulman, *The Balance of Consciousness: Eric Voegelin's Political Theory* (University Park: Pennsylvania State University Press, 1990); Barry Cooper, *Eric Voegelin and the Foundations of Modern Political Science* (Columbia: University of Missouri Press, 1999); Brendan M. Purcell, *The Drama of Humanity: Towards a Philosophy of Humanity in History* (Frankfurt am Main: Peter Lang, 1996); Robert McMahon, "Eric Voegelin's Paradoxes of Consciousness and Participation," *Review of Politics* 61, no. 1 (winter 1999): 117–38; Ellis Sandoz, *The Politics of Truth and Other Untimely Essays: The Crisis of Civic Consciousness* (Columbia: University of Missouri Press, 1999), esp. chap. 10; David Walsh, *Guarded by Mystery: Meaning in a Postmodern Age* (Washington, D.C.: Catholic University of America Press, 1999); Michael Franz, *Eric Voegelin and the Politics of Spiritual Revolt: The Roots of Modern Ideology* (Baton Rouge: Louisiana State University Press, 1992); and Paul Caringella, "Voegelin: Philosopher of Divine Presence," in *Eric Voegelin's Significance for the Modern Mind*, ed. Ellis Sandoz (Baton Rouge: Louisiana State University Press, 1991), 174–205.

ELLIS SANDOZ

IN SEARCH OF ORDER

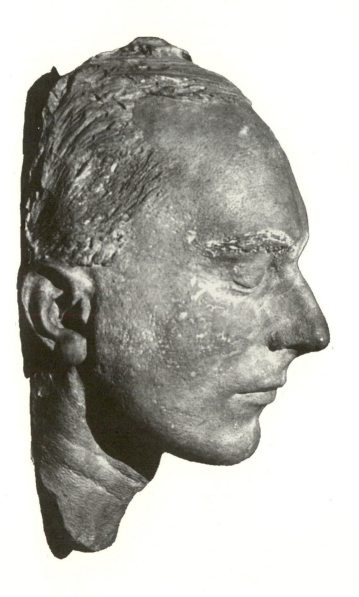

Conigui Dilectissimae

In consideratione creaturatum non est vana et peritura curiositas exercenda; sed gradus ad immortalia et semper manentia faciendus.

(In the study of creature one should not exercise a vain and perishing curiosity, but ascend toward what is immortal and everlasting.)

Saint Augustine, De Vera Religione

ANALYTICAL TABLE OF CONTENTS

9

Foreword

Through the fifty-three years of our marriage I tried to be as much a partner of my husband's life as I could manage to be. It was hard going at first. Because I had no formal academic training I had to get acquainted with his world of learning and thinking. With his guidance I tried to absorb, sometimes only dutifully, but with mounting interest what the world of learning and science had to offer. But since what I have of talents goes more in the direction of loving response, my main and whole interest in life was my husband and his work. I have often been called his silent partner, a title that suits me well and that I would like to keep.

It is only on the insistence of friends that I have agreed to write these lines, to state a few facts that could be of general interest about the origin of this volume. My husband started to write these pages in the summer of 1980 after four years of research, with the devoted assistance of Paul Caringella; and he continued his extensive readings and his writing during the next three years. In late 1983 his health began to fail and the strenuous concentration required for writing became more and more difficult. By that time he had already sent a good part of the manuscript to the Louisiana State University Press, always hoping that some day he would be able to write again. But, as his illness advanced, he finally understood that it was not meant for him to go on living. In his last months I saw him, almost every day, reading and rereading the manuscript, making slight corrections occasionally, and always pointing out to me: This will be volume 5. He liked his work and often talked about it, and he let me know that he knew very well that these pages are the key to all his other works and that in these pages he has gone as far as he could go in analysis, saying what he wanted to say as clearly as it possibly could be said. He did not leave us any instruction concerning publishing; he knew that his work would be in the best and experienced care of Beverly Jarrett, to whom he looked as a friend.

I hope these remarks will be useful for an understanding of this seemingly small volume.

LISSY VOEGELIN

Introduction

An introduction to this final volume of *Order and History* from other hands than Eric Voegelin's, necessitated by his death on January 19, 1985, cannot be the major theoretical statement that introductions to earlier volumes have been. The reader must settle for much less. Moreover, the book itself comes to hand as a fragment, as the unfinished story of the search for order. Our introduction under these circumstances can only be a recollection of Voegelin's path exploring order—and disorder—in history and its reflective rearticulation in his book, with pertinent indication of the new ground broken here.

The fragmentary character of the work before us should not, however, convey a suspicion of its being imperfectly deliberated or lacking revision as a final draft. To the contrary. It is fragmentary only in not extending the analysis to other materials plainly in the author's view and in not illustrating the theoretical presentation in greater detail than he was able to do before time ran out. But the theoretical presentation itself is essentially complete, and the fact that the quest of order is an unfinished story as told by Voegelin is most fitting. For, as he insisted, neither reality nor philosophy can be reduced to a system. Thus, the form of the present work can be said to symbolize Voegelin's philosophical vision of history and comprehensive reality as an unfinished tale, one told by God in the reflective language of spiritually gifted men and women open to the mystery of truth emergent by divine-human encounter in the In-Between of participatory existence, human reality par excellence. Form and content thereby interpenetrate.

The evocation of the participatory reality of the In-Between (or *metaxy*, as Plato called it) is a chief point to be recollected, since it finds expression in the beginning of *Order and History* and remains at the center of Voegelin's search for truth as a differentiating experience-symbol into the present work. Thus, the first paragraph of the introduction to volume I reads as follows:

> God and man, world and society form a primordial community of being. The community with its quaternarian structure is, and is not, a datum of human experience. It is a datum of experience in so far as it is known to man by virtue of his participation in the mystery of its being. It is not a datum of experience in so far as it is not given in the manner of an object of the external world but is knowable only from the perspective of participation in it.

The clarifying exploration continues in subsequent paragraphs. "Participation in being . . . is not a partial involvement of man; he is engaged with the whole of his existence, for participation is existence itself."

> There is an experience of participation, a reflective tension in existence, radiating sense over the proposition: Man, in his existence, participates in being. This sense, however, will turn into nonsense if one forgets that subject and predicate in the proposition are terms which explicate a tension of existence, and are not concepts denoting objects. There is no such thing as a "man" who participates in "being" as if it were an enterprise that he could as well leave alone; there is, rather, a "something," a part of being, capable of experiencing itself as such, and furthermore capable of using language and calling this experiencing consciousness by the name of "man." . . . At the center of his existence man is unknown to himself and must remain so, for the part of being that calls itself man could be known fully only if the community of being and its drama in time were known as a whole. Man's partnership in being is the essence of his existence, and this essence depends on the whole, of which existence is a part. Knowledge of the whole, however, is precluded by the identity of the knower with the partner, and ignorance of the whole precludes essential knowledge of the part. This situation of ignorance with regard to the decisive core of existence is more than disconcerting: it is profoundly disturbing, for from the depth of this ultimate ignorance wells up the anxiety of existence. (*OH*, I:1–2)

Hundreds of pages and eighteen years later, in volume IV of *Order and History* where we left the unfinished story in 1974, Voegelin wrote of the experiential analysis of participation and the truth it discloses in philosophy. The occasion is what he calls the "symbolization of the erotic tension in man's existence as an In-Between reality" conveyed by Plato in the *Symposium*.

The truth of existence in erotic tension [as] conveyed by the prophetess Diotima to Socrates [in the dialogue] . . . is not an information about reality but the event in which the process of reality becomes luminous to itself. It is not an information received, but an insight arising from the dialogue of the soul when it "dialectically" investigates its own suspense "between knowledge and ignorance." When the insight arises, it has the character of the "truth," because it is the exegesis of the erotic tension experienced; but it does arise only when the tension is experienced in such a manner that it breaks forth in its own dialogical exegesis. There is no erotic tension lying around somewhere to be investigated by someone who stumbles on it. The subject-object dichotomy, which is modeled after the cognitive relation between man and things in the external world, does not apply to the event of an "experience-articulating-itself." . . . [Rather, the Socratic dialogue of the soul is] the "event" in which the erotic tension in a man's soul struggles to achieve the articulate luminosity of its own reality. Hence, the dialogue of the soul is not locked up as an event in one person who, after it has happened, informs the rest of mankind of its results as a new doctrine. Though the dialogue occurs in one man's soul, it is not "one man's idea about reality," but an event in the Metaxy where man has "converse" with the divine ground of the process that is common to all men. Because of the divine presence in the dialogue of the *daimonios aner* [spiritual man], the event has a social and historical dimension. The Socratic soul draws into its dialogue the companions and, beyond the immediate companions, all those who are eager to have these dialogues reported to them. The *Symposion* presents itself as the report of a report over intervals of years; and the reporting continues to this day. (*OH*, IV:186)

The sweeping power of Voegelin's meditative language in presenting key dimensions of the participatory reality of the In-Between prepares us for the volume here introduced and also reminds us of two further matters relevant in this context. The first of these is that *resistance* to untruth is the specific origin of the search for truth reflected in Voegelin's philosophy and its exploration of the heights and depths of reality experienced-symbolized. The arcane subject matter and technically abstruse presentation that, as we see in the volume before us, press the limits of language and understanding, must not obscure the existential thrust of the whole enterprise of *Order and History* and its author's heroic efforts in service of truth. "The motivations of my work are simple; they arise from the political situation," Voegelin stated in 1973. The elaboration of resistance to untruth in Plato's philosophy given in many places by Voegelin (for example, the struggle against the sophistic society of the *Republic* analyzed in *Order and History*, III:78–80), is informed by the author's own struggle to find truth amid the corruption of debauched language and ideological politics that began during the 1920s and 1930s in Europe. The "political situation" spoken of, in brief, was that signified by Stalin, Hitler, Mussolini, and the social and intellectual milieux whose historical emergence allowed them to hold sway as representative figures. The passing of these "epigonal" figures from the scene, moreover, did not eradicate the long-term factors that fostered their ascendancy to begin with. Hence, the work of recovering the spiritual ground of existence as a countermove to the degradation of existence crushingly enforced by climates of opinion deformed by ideology and bent on eradication of opposition was a task of both historical understanding and present theoretical urgency. That urgency was memorably expressed in the preface to *Order and History* where Voegelin not only speaks of "amnesia with regard to past achievement" in the quest for order but sternly points to "metastatic faith [as] one of the great sources of disorder, if not the principal one, in the contemporary world" and states that "it is a matter of life and death for all of us to understand the phenomenon and to find remedies against it before it destroys us." He points to philosophical inquiry as one of the modest remedies against the disorders of the time, and writes:

> Ideology is existence in rebellion against God and man. It is the violation of the First and Tenth Commandments, if we want to use the language of Israelite order; it is the *nosos,* the disease of the spirit, if we want to use the language of Aeschylus and Plato. Philosophy is the love of being through the love of divine Being as the source of its order. The Logos of being is the object proper of philosophical inquiry; and the search for truth concerning the order of being cannot be conducted without diagnosing the modes of existence in untruth. The truth of order has to be gained and regained in the perpetual struggle against the fall from it; and the movement toward truth starts from a man's awareness of his existence in untruth. The diagnostic and therapeutic functions are inseparable in philosophy as a form of existence. (*OH,* I:ix–xiv)

Order and History, thus, was conceived as diagnosis of and therapy for troubled times, intended to help establish an island "of order in the disorder of the age."

A second matter called to mind by the passages reflecting the participatory reality of the In-Between is the primacy of the symbol God. It is the first word in the body of the book, and it synonymously appears as the "divine ground" and "spiritual man" in the analysis of the *Symposium* quoted earlier. Philosophy itself, as we just saw, is "the love of being through the love of divine Being" as its source of order. In the turning-about of the whole man, Eric Voegelin, away from the shadows of ideological deception and toward the light of truth that somehow attracted him, the exigency of personal resistance to National Socialist untruth with its blanket claims on human existence forced a recovery of the classic and Christian science of man as the way of conducting his critique of modernity and reorienting himself in reality. As the evocation of Plato's Parable of the Cave implies, the interest in God was primarily philosophical and existential rather than "religious," in the sense of doctrines, dogmas, and creeds. The appeal beyond comprehensive claims of political truth lies to "the Laws of Nature and of Nature's God," Voegelin discovered in his first trip to America in 1924; and he linked the commonsense philosophy of the Scottish Enlightenment adumbrated in American thought with the insights of Hellenic rationality as contained in the writings of Plato and Aristotle, who evoke the transcendent divine Ground, Beauty, Good, and the Prime Mover as the source of being and order. Voegelin began to learn Greek in Vienna in the early 1930s so as to read the key source materials; after fleeing the Nazis and moving permanently to America, he began to study Hebrew with a rabbi in Tuscaloosa, Alabama, in about 1940, so as to read the Old Testament.

Long before the first lines of *Order and History* were written, Voegelin energetically stressed, in correspondence with his great friend Alfred Schütz in 1943, that (in contrast to Edmund Husserl's immanentism) the "philosophical problems of transcendence [were] the decisive problems of philosophy" (*Anamnesis* [1966], 36). He reiterated the view a decade later when, in another letter to the same correspondent, replying to questions about his new book, *The New Science of Politics* [1952], Voegelin wrote as follows:

> And now to your decisive question: is theory possible only within the framework of Christianity? Quite obviously not. Greek philosophy is pre-Christian, yet one can philosophize perfectly well as a Platonist or an Aristotelian. Philosophizing seems to me to be in essence the interpretation of experiences of transcendence; these experiences have, as an historical fact, existed independently of Christianity, and there is no question that today too it is equally possible to philosophize without Christianity. But this basic and unequivocal answer must be

qualified on one essential point. There are degrees of differentiation of experiences. I would take it as a principle of philosophizing that the philosopher must include in his interpretation the maximally differentiated experiences. . . . Now with Christianity a decisive differentiation has occurred. (Quoted from Peter J. Opitz and Gregor Sebba, eds., *The Philosophy of Order* [1981], 450)

This, then, brings us to the book before us. For the concluding volume of *Order and History* is devoted to the elucidation of the experiences of transcendence that Voegelin has widely discussed in previous volumes and in essays and books not included in this work. There can be no doubt that Voegelin held true to his view that "philosophizing seems to me to be in essence the interpretation of experiences of transcendence," expressed to Schütz decades earlier. Precisely how this completes the work and the noetic science comprising a new philosophy of consciousness, politics, and history is a vast subject best left to the commentators and to another place. Briefly, since experiences of transcendence compose the essence of both philosophy and the order of human existence and history, it remains to be shown in a theoretically acute manner exactly what such experiences are. This is the essential task of the present volume. A few words clarifying the context of Voegelin's remarkable effort in finally discharging that task can conclude this introduction to the capstone of the noetic science of human affairs that subtly revises and critically supplants in significant respects the traditional ontology and epistemology of philosophy.

A particularly alarming page of that generally disturbing prolegomenon to *Order and History* published as *The New Science of Politics* prefigures the meditative preoccupation of the author's final decade of work, especially as that comes to fruition with *In Search of Order*. In discussing the drive for existential certainty that partly explains the commission of fallaciously immanentizing Christian eschatological faith symbolisms by modern Gnostics, Voegelin reflects on the lust for massive certainty and its relative absence in the delicate texture of the faith-grace relationship. He writes:

Uncertainty is the very essence of Christianity. The feeling of security in a "world full of gods" [provided by the old cosmological mythical religions] is lost with the gods themselves; when the world is de-divinized, communication with the world-transcendent God is reduced to the tenuous bond of faith, in the sense of Heb. 11:1, as the substance of things hoped for and the proof of things unseen.

20

> Ontologically, the substance of things hoped for is nowhere to be found but in faith itself; and, epistemologically, there is no proof for things unseen but again this very faith. The bond is tenuous, indeed, and it may snap easily. The life of the soul in openness toward God, the waiting, the periods of aridity and dullness, guilt and despondency, contrition and repentance, forsakenness and hope against hope, the silent stirrings of love and grace, trembling on the verge of a certainty which if gained is loss—the very lightness of this fabric may prove too heavy a burden for men who lust for massively possessive experience. (*NSP*, 122)

What a rather defensive footnote identifies as "a psychology of experience"—not the theology or dogmatics of faith—is Voegelin's subject in these lines and, broadly, also in the present work. That there is anything uncertain about their faith came as unwelcome news, however, to dogmatic Christians who reacted angrily to the suggestion, both in 1952 and on later similar occasions, such as in the analysis of Paul's faith in *The Ecumenic Age* (*OH*, IV:239–71). Not merely the Gnostic-ideologues but the faithful contribute to the vexed "dogmatomachy" of the age, and Voegelin's purpose in seeking to recapture the experiential foundations of civilization through impartial and searching analysis made him, in varying degrees, to be sure, the adversary of all parties bent on success in the power struggle and the butt of their uncomprehending and uncaring obloquy when he would not be recruited to their causes.

The personal, social, and historical dimensions of the philosopher's vocation come to view in a pertinent way from these last reflections. Intent upon the crucial formative experiences-symbolisms, of whatever ambience, that have happened in the time-eternity of the human-divine reality of the In-Between called history, the man who is the site of experience-articulating-itself (now or in the past) both is and is not bound by his individual identity, ethnic and national membership, and the historical circumstances of his life. The paradoxes of the quest, just hinted in the dyadic and triadic hyphenated terms, form a major subject of the pages ahead. The Archimedean point to view reality "objectively" that is nowhere to be found is matched by the pure experience-symbol that is equally inaccessible in the ineluctably participatory and particular reality of even the most sensitive and acute explorers of noetic and pneumatic truth.

The vast enterprise of elaborating a theory of order and history is not abandoned by Voegelin in concluding the work with this slender volume. But that theory forms in ways that Voegelin thought would surprise some readers. In the seventeen years separating publication of the first three and the fourth volumes of *Order and History* (1956–1957 to 1974), the underlying philosophy of consciousness presupposed in the earlier work (and of concern all the way back to the author's first book in 1928) appeared full blown in 1966 in *Anamnesis*. In the thirteen years since the publication of the fourth volume itself, and preceding and paralleling its publication, other writings and publications have developed vital lines of inquiry completed by Voegelin herein. Among the most essential of these essays are "The Beginning and the Beyond" (written between 1975 and 1978, a seventy-page typescript left unfinished and unpublished), and published essays that include "Immortality: Experience and Symbol" (1967); "Equivalences of Experience and Symbolization in History" (1970); "The Gospel and Culture" (1971); "On Hegel: A Study in Sorcery" (1971); "Reason: The Classic Experience" (1974); "Remembrance of Things Past" (1978); "Wisdom and the Magic of the Extreme: A Meditation" (1981); and the valedictory "Quod Deus Dicitur" (1986), dictated from his death bed.[1] These essays, among others, are reprinted in volumes 12 and 28 of the *Collected Works of Eric Voegelin*. Some of these essays, along with others not mentioned, were at one time or another intended for possible inclusion in this volume; but that intention changed as the conception of the book itself modified in the author's thinking, and there is no way

1. A bibliography of Voegelin's writings down to 1981 can be found in Ellis Sandoz, *The Voegelinian Revolution: A Biographical Introduction* (1981; 2nd ed., New Brunswick: Transaction Publishers, 2000). "Quod Deus Dicitur" was published in the *Journal of the American Academy of Religion* 53, no. 3 (1985): 569–84, and incorporates about ten pages of the unpublished "The Beginning and the Beyond." Citations for the Voegelin articles mentioned in the text are as follows: "Immortality: Experience and Symbol," *Harvard Theological Review* 60 (1967): 235–79; "Equivalences of Experience and Symbolization in History," in *Eternita è Storia: I valori permanenti nel divenire storico* (Florence: Valecchi, 1970), 215–34 (reprinted in *Philosophical Studies* 28 [n.d.]: 88–103; "The Gospel and Culture," in *Jesus and Man's Hope*, ed. Donald G. Miller and Dikran Y. Hadidian, 2 vols. (Pittsburgh: Pittsburgh Theological Seminary Press, 1971), 2:59–101; "On Hegel: A Study in Sorcery," *Studium Generale* 24 (1971): 335–68 (reprinted in J. T. Fraser et al., eds., *The Study of Time* [Heidelberg, 1972], 418–51; "Reason: The Classic Experience," *Southern Review* n.s. 10 (1974): 237–64; "Remembrance of Things Past," in *Anamnesis*, ed. and trans. Gerhart Niemeyer (Notre Dame: University of Notre Dame Press, 1978), 3–13; "Wisdom and the Magic of the Extreme: A Meditation," *Southern Review* n.s. 17 (1981): 235–87. In addition, "Response to Professor Altizer's 'A New History and a New but Ancient God?'" *Journal of the American Academy of Religion* 43 (1975): 765–72. All of these essays are reprinted in *Published Essays, 1966–1985*, ed. Ellis Sandoz, vol. 12 of *The Collected Works of Eric Voegelin* (1990; available, Columbia: University of Missouri Press, 1999). The series is hereinafter abbreviated *CW*.

of knowing with certainty how the book would have appeared had Voegelin himself lived to see it through the press. It is obvious, however, that "The Beginning and the Beyond" and "Wisdom and the Magic of the Extreme," together with "Quod Deus Dicitur," belong to the same meditative horizon as the manuscript published here.

The theory of order and history that Voegelin hoped to find through the study of the history of order when he set out on the quest over thirty years ago was undertaken in the conviction, as we have recalled, that the interpretation of experiences of transcendence is the heart of philosophizing. With due allowance made for the richness and subtlety of the analysis that carefully assays the multifaceted reality of power politics, historiography, and spiritual outbursts as major structures inextricably bound together in the process of reality and demanding balanced treatment in a philosophy of consciousness and history, as emphasized in volume IV, the heart of the matter remains with the experiences of transcendence. And a thoroughly elaborated theory has emerged in a powerful presentation that transforms the terms of the debate here just as they were transformed by the abandonment of the original conception of the book itself. The pluralistic field of the history of universal mankind forced abandonment of the originally projected six-volume work reflecting a unilinear conception of history and unfolding consciousness. The stages announced in *The New Science of Politics* in 1952 of theoretical differentiation proceeding from the cosmological to the anthropological to the soteriological were already in the background when *Israel and Revelation* appeared in 1956. The crisp distinction between the revelatory or pneumatic experiences reflected in the Old Testament and Christianity as God in search of man, in contrast to those of philosophy or noetic experiences when the accent falls on man in search of God, became less marked. It was found that revelation and reason could not be so partitioned for, indeed, reason was itself a revelation in the psyche of the Greek philosophers, especially Plato, and that noetic analysis was common to the New Testament and to philosophy. Moreover, although warned against in the first paragraph of the book, as we noticed, the language of thingness and of cognitive subjects apprehending objects, even if understood metaphorically, remains too present in an analysis that habitually identifies immanent and transcendent reality as entities, perhaps as man seeking God, or God in search of man. The "intentionalist fallacy" still lurks in the wings deforming experience. To overcome it the philosophy of consciousness has to be developed, and within that, the ontic and cognitive dimensions of the experiences themselves analyzed.

But where and how? *Only* in the concrete consciousness of the concrete persons in whom the experiences come to articulation. Voegelin repeatedly stresses, as in the comments on the *Symposium* quoted earlier, "there is no erotic tension lying around somewhere to be investigated by someone who stumbles on it." The remainder of the passage can be consulted. Herein lies the sole and precious foundation in empirical evidence of noetic science, of the critical reflective understanding of reality attainable in the kind of meditative and imaginative vision called philosophy, if the term be accorded Plato's meaning of it. In "The Beginning and the Beyond," after considering the concrete instances of a variety of contemplative horizons, including the Vedic, philosophic, prophetic, and apostolic, Voegelin summarizes:

> I have traced the consciousness of language through a number of representative cases in the period of the great differentiations. The variants of consciousness reach from the Vedic outburst of the comprehensive reality into self-illuminating speech, to the emergence of the word from the Metaxy of the psyche, further to its emergence from the personal encounter of the prophet with God and its imaginative transformation into the ambiguous word of Scripture, and finally to the epiphany of Christ with its insight into man as the acting, suffering, and ultimately victorious partner in a process in which reality becomes luminous for its divine mystery through the truth of language. Although the variants cover a wide range on the scale of compactness and differentiation, the spiritualists who go through the experience all agree on the sacrality of a language in which the truth of divine reality becomes articulate. The experience and the language of truth belong together as parts of a process that derives its sacrality from the flux of divine presence in it. It will now be possible to give precision to some of the insights implied in the process as it presents itself empirically.
>
> The most serious obstacle to a proper understanding of the experience . . . is the penchant to hypostatize. The object in the world of sense perception has become so forcefully the model of "things" that it intrudes itself inadvertently into the understanding of experiences that are not concerned with objects but with the mystery of a reality in which the objects of the external world are to be found among other "things." The experience of divine reality, it is true, occurs in the psyche of a man who is solidly rooted by his body in the external world, but the psyche itself exists in the Metaxy, in the tension toward the divine ground of being. It is the sensorium for divine reality and

24

the site of its luminous presence. Even more, it is the site in which the comprehensive reality becomes luminous to itself and engenders the language in which we speak of a reality that comprehends both an external world and the mystery of its Beginning and Beyond, as well as the metaleptic psyche in which the experience occurs and engenders its language. In the experience not only the truth of divine reality becomes luminous but, at the same time, the truth of the world in which the experience occurs. There is no "external" or "immanent" world unless it is recognized as such by its relation to something that is "internal" or "transcendent." Such terms as *immanent* and *transcendent*, *external* and *internal*, *this world* and *the other world*, and so forth, do not denote objects or their properties but are the language indices arising from the Metaxy in the event of its becoming luminous for the comprehensive reality, its structure and dynamics. The terms are exegetic, not descriptive. They indicate the movements of the soul when, in the Metaxy of consciousness, it explores the experience of divine reality and tries to find the language that will articulate its exegetic movements. Hence, the language and its truth engendered by the event do not refer to an outside object, but are the language and truth of reality as it becomes luminous in man's consciousness. On another occasion I have concentrated this problem in the statement: The fact of revelation is its content. [Cf. *NSP*, 78]

Since the experience has no content but itself, the miracle of reality breaking forth into the language of its truth will move into the center of attention when consciousness differentiates sufficiently to become luminous for its own movements. The language of truth about reality tends historically to be recognized as the truth of language in reality. An important phase in this process is represented by the cosmogony of Genesis. The creation story lets the cosmos, with its hierarchy of being from the inorganic universe, through vegetable and animal life, to man, be spoken into existence by God. Reality is a story spoken in the creative language of God; and in one of its figures, in man who is created in the image of God, reality responds to the mystery of the creative word with the truth of the creation story. Or inversely, from the human side, divine reality must be symbolized analogically as the creative word of God because the experience engenders for its expression the imaginative word of the cosmogonic myth. Reality is an act of divine mythopoesis that becomes luminous for its truth when it evokes the responsive myth from man's experience. This perfect correlation between the language of truth and the truth of language in reality . . . is the distinguishing mark of the creation story.[2]

This quotation will perhaps provide the reader with a perspective on the book to follow that will enhance its accessibility, even if this

2. "The Beginning and the Beyond," in *What Is History? and Other Late Unpublished Writings*, ed. Thomas A. Hollweck and Paul Caringella, vol. 28 of *CW*, 184–86.

is a first acquaintance with Voegelin. The book's opening meditation on "The Beginning of the Beginning" turns to an exploration of Genesis and unfolds an analysis of the paradox of consciousness and the complex of consciousness-reality-language as the texture of experience symbolized imaginatively, with attention to the truth and its deformation. Thereafter, "Reflective Distance *vs*. Reflective Identity" investigates the deformative and formative forces at work in modern philosophy, with particular attention to Hegel and the German revolution of consciousness; it then turns to Hesiod and to Plato's struggle for a language of existential consciousness, especially as presented in the *Timaeus*.

Voegelin's finding and refining the content of truth articulated over millennia, in an activity whose terms must be applied reflexively to itself as reality becoming luminous in our own present, was once characterized to me in these words: "From my first contact with such works as the *Cloud of Unknowing*, to my more recent understanding of the mystical problem . . . the great issue [has been]: not to stop at what may be called classical mysticism, but to restore the problem of the Metaxy for society and history."[3] This introduction to volume V will have served its purpose if something of the final shape of Voegelin's restorative work has come to view in these pages whose adequacy depends upon my collaboration with the author in trying to remember what ought not be forgotten.

ELLIS SANDOZ

---

3. Eric Voegelin to Ellis Sandoz, December 30, 1971, in Eric Voegelin Papers, Hoover Institution Library, Stanford University, box 27.10.

1

⟡

The Beginning of the Beginning

§1. Where Does the Beginning Begin?

As I am putting down these words on an empty page I have begun to write a sentence that, when it is finished, will be the beginning of a chapter on certain problems of Beginning.

The sentence is finished. But is it true?

The reader does not know whether it is true before he has finished reading the chapter and can judge whether it is indeed a sermon on the sentence as its text. Nor do I know at this time, for the chapter is yet unwritten; and although I have a general idea of its construction, I know from experience that new ideas have a habit of emerging while the writing is going on, compelling changes in the construction and making the beginning unsuitable. Unless we want to enjoy the delights of a Sternean stream of consciousness, the story has no beginning before it has come to its end. What then comes first: the beginning or the end?

Neither the beginning nor the end comes first. The question rather points to whole, a thing called "chapter," with a variety of dimensions. This whole has an extension in space as a body of letters written or printed as pages. It then has a temporal dimension in the process of being written or being read. And finally it has a dimension of meaning, neither spatial nor temporal, in the existential process of the quest for truth in which both the reader and the writer are engaged. Is then the whole, with its spatio-temporal and existential dimensions, the answer to the question: What comes first?

The whole as a literary unit called "chapter" is not the answer either. By its character of a chapter in a book, the whole points beyond itself to the intricate problems of communication between reader and writer. The book is meant to be read; it is an event in

27

a vast social field of thought and language, of writing and reading about matters that the members of the field believe to be of concern for their existence in truth. The whole is no beginning in an absolute sense; it is no beginning of anything at all unless it has a function in a communion of existential concern; and the communion of concern as a social field depends for its existence on the communicability of the concern through language. Back we are referred, the reader and I, to the words, for they have begun before I have begun to put them down. Was the word in the beginning after all?

Well, in order to convey its meaning, the chapter must be intelligible; it must be written in a language common to reader and writer, in this case English; and this language must be written according to contemporary standards of word usage, grammar, sentence building, punctuation, paragraphing, so that the reader will not encounter improper obstacles to his effort of understanding the chapter's meaning. But that is not enough. For the chapter is not a piece of information about familiar objects of the external world; rather, it seeks to communicate an act of participation in the quest for truth. Besides satisfying standards of intelligibility in the everyday sense of reference to objects, the language must be common in the sense of communicating the meanings in the area of the existential quest; it must be able to convey the meanings of a philosopher's experience, meditation, and exegetic analysis. This philosopher's language, however, does not begin with the present chapter either, but has been structured by a millennial history of the philosophers' quest for truth, a history that has not stopped at some point in the past but is continuing in the present effort between reader and writer. The social field constituted by the philosophers' language, thus, is not limited to communication through the spoken and written word among contemporaries, but extends historically from a distant past, through the present, into the future.

§2. The Paradox of Consciousness

By now the Beginning has wandered from the opening of the chapter to its end, from the end of the chapter to its whole, from the whole to the English language as the means of communication between reader and writer, and from the process of communication in English to a philosophers' language that communicates among the participants in the millennial process of the quest for truth. And still the way of the beginning has not reached the end that would be intelligible as its true beginning; for the appearance of a "philosophers' language" raises new questions concerning a problem that begins to look rather like a complex of problems. There is something peculiar about the "philosophers' language": In order to be intelligible, it had to be spoken in one of the several ethnic, imperial, and national languages that have developed ever since antiquity, although it does not seem to be identical with any one of them; and yet, while it is not identical with any one of the considerable number of ancient and modern languages in which it has been spoken, they all have left, and are leaving, their specific traces of meaning in the language used, and expected to be understood, in the present chapter; but then again, in its millennial course the quest for truth has developed, and is still developing, a language of its own. What is the structure in reality that will induce, when experienced, this equivocal use of the term "language"?

The equivocation is induced by the paradoxical structure of consciousness and its relation to reality. On the one hand, we speak of consciousness as a something located in human beings in their bodily existence. In relation to this concretely embodied consciousness, reality assumes the position of an object intended. Moreover, by its position as an object intended by a consciousness that is bodily located, reality itself acquires a metaphorical touch of external thingness. We use this metaphor in such phrases as "being conscious of something," "remembering or imagining something," "thinking about something," "studying or exploring something." I shall, therefore, call this structure of consciousness its intentionality, and the corresponding structure of reality its thingness. On the other hand, we know the bodily located consciousness to be also real; and this concretely located consciousness does not belong to another genus of reality, but is part of the same reality that has moved, in its relation to man's consciousness, into the position of a thing-reality. In this second sense, then, reality is not an object of consciousness but the something in which consciousness occurs as an event of participation between partners in the community of being.

In the complex experience, presently in process of articulation, reality moves from the position of an intended object to that of a subject, while the consciousness of the human subject intending objects moves to the position of a predicative event in the subject "reality" as it becomes luminous for its truth. Consciousness, thus, has the structural aspect not only of intentionality but also of luminosity. Moreover, when consciousness is experienced as an event of participatory illumination in the reality that comprehends the partners to the event, it has to be located, not in one of the partners, but in the comprehending reality; consciousness has a structural dimension by which it belongs, not to man in his bodily existence, but to the reality in which man, the other partners to the community of being, and the participatory relations among them occur. If the spatial metaphor be still permitted, the luminosity of consciousness is located somewhere "between" human consciousness in bodily existence and reality intended in its mode of thingness.

Contemporary philosophical discourse has no conventionally accepted language for the structures just analyzed. Hence, to denote the between-status of consciousness I shall use the Greek work *metaxy*, developed by Plato as the technical term in his analysis of the structure. To denote the reality that comprehends the partners in being, i.e., God and the world, man and society, no technical term has been developed, as far as I know, by anybody. However, I notice that philosophers, when they run into this structure incidentally in their exploration of other subject matters, have a habit of referring to it by a neutral "it." The It referred to is the mysterious "it" that also occurs in everyday language in such phrases as "it rains." I shall call it therefore the It-reality, as distinguished from the thing-reality.

The equivocal use of the word "language" pointed toward an experience of reality that would have to express itself by this usage; and the quest proceeded to the structure of consciousness as the experience engendering the equivocation. But is this answer a step closer to the Beginning? At first sight it rather looks like an expansion of equivocations. There is a consciousness with two structural meanings, to be distinguished as intentionality and luminosity. There is a reality with two structural meanings, to be distinguished as the thing-reality and the It-reality. Consciousness, then, is a subject intending reality as its object, but at the same time a something in a comprehending reality; and reality is the object of consciousness, but at the same time the subject of which consciousness is to be predicated. Where in this complex of equivocations do we find a beginning?

§3. The Complex of Consciousness-Reality-Language

There is indeed no beginning to be found in this or that part of the complex; the beginning will reveal itself only if the paradox is taken seriously as the something that constitutes the complex as a whole. This complex, however, as the expansion of equivocations shows, includes language and truth, together with consciousness and reality. There is no autonomous, nonparadoxic language, ready to be used by man as a system of signs when he wants to refer to the paradoxic structures of reality and consciousness. Words and their meanings are just as much a part of the reality to which they refer as the being things are partners in the comprehending reality; language participates in the paradox of a quest that lets reality become luminous for its truth by pursuing truth as a thing tended. This paradoxic structure of language has caused certain questions, controversies, and terminological difficulties to become constants in the philosophers' discourse since antiquity without approaching satisfactory conclusions.

One such constant is the great question whether language is "conventional" or "natural." The conventionalist opinion, today the more fashionable one, is moved by the intentionality of consciousness and the corresponding thing-reality to regard words as phonic signs, more or less arbitrarily chosen to refer to things. The naturalists are moved by a sense that signs must have some sort of reality in common with the things to which they refer, or they would not be intelligible as signs with certain meanings. Both of the opinions are precariously founded because their adherents were not present when language originated, while the men who were present left no record of the event but language itself. As I understand the issue, both groups are right in their motivations, as well as in their attempts to explore the conditions incidental to the origin of language and its meaning; and yet both are wrong inasmuch as they disregard the fact that the epiphany of structures in reality—be they atoms, molecules, genes, biological species, races, human consciousness, or language—is a mystery inaccessible to explanation.

Another such constant is the distinction between "concept" and "symbol," with the difficulty of assigning precise meanings to the terms. This problem has plagued the philosophers' discourse ever since Plato recognized it and, in the practice of his own philosophizing, coped with it by using both conceptual analysis and mythic symbolization as complementary modes of thought in the quest for truth. In the so-called modern centuries, since the Renaissance, these difficulties have become further aggravated by the parallel growth of the natural and the historical sciences. On the one hand, the advance of the natural sciences concentrated attention intensely on the particular problems of conceptualization they posed, so intensely indeed that the concentration has become the motivating force of a socially still-expanding movement of sectarians who want to monopolize the meaning of the terms "truth" and "science" for the results and methods of the mathematizing sciences. On the other hand, the equally astounding advance of the historical sciences has concentrated attention on the problems of symbolization posed by the discoveries in the ancient civilizations and their mythologies, as well as by the exploration of the modes of thought to be found in contemporary tribal societies. Again the two concentrations are transparent for the experiences of intentionality and luminosity, of thing-reality and It-reality, behind them; again the representatives of both concentrations are right in their pursuit of truth as long as they confine themselves to areas of reality in which the structures of their preference predominate; and again both are wrong when they engage in magic dreams of a truth that can be reached by concentrating exclusively on either the intentionality of conceptualizing science or the luminosity of mythic and revelatory symbols.

From the analysis there emerges the complex of consciousness-reality-language as a something that receives its character as a unit through the pervasive presence of another something, called the paradox of intentionality and luminosity, of thing-ness and It-ness. In what sense, however, is this complex the beginning we, the reader and I, are pursuing without having found it yet? And what are such terms and phrases as "complex," "paradox," and "pervasive presence"? Are they concepts intending a thing-reality or are they symbols expressing the It-reality? or are they both? or are they perhaps no more than pieces of empty talk? Do all these things really exist anywhere as a meaningful complex except in the phantasy of the present analysis? What is needed to calm down this class of questions is a literary document, a concrete case, which intelligibly demonstrates the co-existence of the structures in the unit of the complex, as well as the meaning of this complex as a "beginning." For this purpose I shall present one of the classic cases where the Beginning makes its beginning with precisely the complex of structures under analysis, the case of Genesis 1.

§4. The Beginning of Genesis 1

In Genesis 1:1, we read: "In the beginning God created the heavens and the earth." We can hardly come closer to the real beginning of anything than in an original act of creating everything. But what is creation? and how does God proceed when he creates? Genesis 1:3 gives this information: "And God said, 'Let there be light'; and there was light" or, in the more literal Buber-Rosenzweig translation, "God spoke: Light be! Light became." The reality light appears in this verse when the divine command calls it forth, into its existential luminosity, by calling it by its name. The spoken word, it appears, is more than a mere sign signifying something; it is a power in reality that evokes structures in reality by naming them. This magic power of the word can be discerned even more clearly in Genesis 1:5 (Buber-Rosenzweig translation): "God called to light: Day! and to the darkness he called: Night! And there became evening and morning: A Day."

Still, the power of the creative word is not yet the true beginning we are pursuing; for the account of the creative process is inherently incomplete. It forcefully raises such questions as: To whom are the divine commands addressed? and who is the God who addresses them? or what is that kind of reality where the spoken word evokes the structures of which it speaks? In the situation created by these questions, a recourse to theological conceptions of "revelation" would be of little help, for even a revelation must make sense as a spoken or written word, a word heard or seen, if the message the word reveals is to be intelligible. The authors of Genesis 1, we prefer to assume, were human beings of the same kind as we are; they had to face the same kind of reality, with the same kind of consciousness, as we do; and when, in their pursuit of truth, they put down their words on whatever material, they had to raise, and to cope with, the same questions we confront when we put down our words. In the situation created by the question What is that kind of reality where the spoken word evokes the structures of which it speaks? they had to find the language symbols that would adequately express the experience and structure of what I have called the It-reality. How did they do it? The answer is given by Genesis 1:2: "The earth was waste and void; darkness was on the face of the deep; and the spirit [breath] of God was moving over the face of the water." Over an emptiness, over a formless waste of something there moves, perhaps like a storm, the breath or spirit, the *ruach*, of God, or rather of a plural divinity, *elohim*. The It-reality, thus, is symbolized as the strong movement of a spiritual consciousness, imposing form on a formless and nonforming countermovement, as the tension between a pneumatic, formative force (*ruach*; in later Greek translation, *pneuma*) and an at least passively resistant counterforce. Moreover, the tension in the It is definitely not the tension of a human consciousness in its struggle with reality for its truth; it is recognized as a nonhuman process, to be symbolized as divine; and yet it has to convey an aura of analogy with the human process because man experiences his own acts, such as the quest for truth, as acts of participation in the process of the It. When the authors of Genesis 1 put down the first words of their text they were conscious of beginning an act of participation in the mysterious Beginning of the It.

Digression on Conventional Misunderstandings

In the intellectual climate of our time, the experienced tensions of consciousness, their expression through symbols, and their differentiating exploration are exposed to certain misunderstandings. At this point it will be prudent to mention some of them; by warding them off it will be possible to clarify the structure of the present quest still further:

(1) One source of misunderstandings is the various psychologies of projection. The symbolism of Genesis 1 must not be misconstrued as an "anthropomorphism," or the projection of a human into a divine consciousness; nor would the opposite misconstruction as a "theomorphism," or a projection of divine into human consciousness, be admissible. On principle, the poles of an experienced tension must not be deformed into entities existing apart from the tension experienced; the tension itself is the structure to

be explored; it must not be fragmentized for the purpose of using one of the poles as the basis for clever psychologizing. That is not to say that projections do not really occur; on the contrary, they occur quite frequently, but as secondary phenomena, be it the humanization of gods or the divinization of men. One such phenomenon is the Feuerbach-Marx divinization of man for the purpose of explaining divine reality as a human projection that, if returned to man, will produce full humanity. Such charges, however, cannot be laid against a pneumatically differentiated search of the Beginning like Genesis 1, for every man is really conscious of participating in a process that does not begin with the participants but with the mysterious It that encompasses them all.

(2) The present analysis should not be misunderstood as a contribution to the great historiographic enterprises of comparative religion and comparative mythology. The historiographic results are presupposed and gratefully accepted, but in the present context they are submitted to philosophic analysis. It would not be helpful, but rather would divert attention from the characteristics of Genesis 1, if I were to indulge in an extensive account of "influences," such as the Egyptian and Babylonian antecedents of the mythical symbols employed. The knowledge of these antecedents certainly is of the first importance for understanding the historical situation of the authors, of the cultural environment in which they moved, and of the language they had to speak in their own mythospeculative enterprise. This knowledge, however, is now submitted to categorization in terms of the philosophers' language. Moreover, the "philosophers' language" appears to have a habit of multiplying languages as soon as it touches the historical materials. We had to speak of a language of the "myth," of "mythospeculations" within a general mythic language; and now we must speak of Genesis 1 as a "pneumatically differentiated mythospeculation," if we want to understand the differentiated use to which the language of the myth was put in Genesis, creating by this use a new language for new insights. This manifold of languages must be accepted as a structure in the history of the quest for truth. The languages are all recognizable and intelligible as languages because, in their various modes of experiential compactness and differentiation, they all symbolize the same structures of consciousness that, in a more differentiated mode, are symbolized in the philosophers' quest for truth. Their plurality, in the parallels and the sequences of the manifold, reveals

language as an integral part of the complex consciousness-reality-language, pervaded by the paradox of intentionality and luminosity, in its historical unfolding of the truth of reality. The language symbols unfold as part of the unfolding truth of reality. This philosophers' understanding of language must not be confused with the linguists' conception of language as a system of signs. But that should be obvious enough not to require further elaboration.

(3) And finally, the analysis should not be misunderstood as a doctrinal exegesis in the sense of later, ecclesiastic theologies. At present we are not interested in the question whether the doctrine of a *creatio ex nihilo* is the most suitable interpretation of Genesis 1 or not; nor in the millennial question of why a creation that its Creator found "good" should require salvational interventions to redeem it from its evil. Rather, we are interested in the experience of the It that was symbolized by the authors of Genesis; and they experienced the Beginning as an evocation, by the force of the pneumatic word, of form in reality from a formless, unstructured waste. This formless waste, then, must be guarded against the conventional misunderstandings of a modernist mind that is accustomed to think of It-reality in terms of thing-reality. For this formless waste is neither nothing nor not-nothing: (a) It is not nothing, for if it were nothing, no creative evocation of something would be necessary; the formed reality would be there already. (b) And yet, it is nothing, if by something is meant any structure experienced as real in postcreational reality; the formless waste is not a "matter" on which the pneumatic Creator works, if by "matter" is understood anything that we call matter in everyday life or in physics. The symbolism of this peculiar precreational stuff or material, which is not a structured, postcreational matter, will perhaps come closer to our understanding when we remember that our "matter" derives from the Latin *materia*, which in turn derives from *mater*, the originally generating maternal reality. The formless waste (*tohu*) of Genesis has preserved, probably through its relation to the Babylonian *tiamat*, the mythic meaning of feminine productivity in the act of generation. But then again, this piece of historical information must not be used to misconstrue the story of Genesis as a "sublimated" version of creation through a sex act, perhaps by imposing some psychoanalytic interpretation. A reductionist construction of this type would destroy both the differentiating achievement of

Genesis and the meaning of the myth. For the authors of Genesis, having differentiated the formative force in the It as the evocative power of the spirit and its word, had to differentiate a formless waste over the depth as the correlative recipient of the formative command, if they wanted to understand the It as the Beginning of their experienced struggle for spiritual order in man, society, and history. By differentiating the pneumatic struggle as the Beginning of the mysterious epiphany of all structure in reality, however, they revealed the presence of its consciousness in the compact language of earlier mythospeculations on the Beginning, such as the various cosmogonies, anthropogonies, and theogonies. If these fundamental issues are obscured by conventional misunderstandings, we lose the understanding of Genesis as one of the great documents in the historical process of advance from compact to differentiated consciousness and the corresponding advance from compact to differentiated languages. If we lose this understanding, we furthermore lose the larger historical horizon of the differentiating advances, as for instance the equivalences between the symbolization of the Beginning in Genesis and its symbolization as the imposition of form on a formless *chora* in Plato's *Timaeus*. And if we lose the larger historical horizon of the advances, finally, we lose the possibility of recognizing in the pneumatic differentiation of Genesis the compact presence of the noetic structure of consciousness, the presence of the complex consciousness-reality-language.

The contemporary climate of opinion has created a social field of considerable power; anybody who dares to think within the range of its pressure has to reckon with its various antagonisms to thought. The antagonisms are not thought through, or they would not exist; they derive their social force from having become habitual to the degree of an automatism. Assuming that the reader, in his effort to understand the present analysis, is laboring under the same pressures as I am in conducting it and writing it out, I have articulated in the preceding pages some of the inarticulate pressures on the quest for truth in our time. I hope the brief sketch is sufficient, not only to ward off the specific misunderstandings mentioned, but to bring the general issue to attention, so that further interruptions of the analysis for this purpose will become unnecessary. I shall now resume the analysis at the point it had reached before this digression on conventional misunderstandings.

§5. The True Story

The authors of Genesis 1, as I said, were conscious of beginning an act of participation in the mysterious Beginning of the It, when they put down the first words of their text. As a literary document, the text is to be dated in post-Exilic times, somewhere between the middle of the sixth and the middle of the fifth centuries B.C. It opens a story of mankind from its beginning in Creation, through the history of the Patriarchs, of captivity and Exodus, of Palestinian settlement, of the Davidic-Solomonic empire, of the kingdoms and their catastrophe, of Exile and return, down to the Deutero-Isaianic dream of a world-Israel, under the guidance of God's covenants with man. Through Israel, the history of man continues the creational process of order in reality; it is part of the comprehending story of the It; and the point at which the story arrives in the event of Genesis derives its significance from the revelation of the truth that the epiphany of structure in reality culminates in the attunement of human history to the command of the pneumatic Word.

The story and the truth it is meant to convey are clearly told, but what do the story and its truth mean in terms of experience and symbolization?

The quest for truth, it appears, does not result in a piece of information that would have been available at other times and in other situations or that, when found, would be unqualifiedly valid in its specific form for all future times in all future situations. The event of the quest is part of a story told by the It, and yet a story to be told by the human questioner, if he wants to articulate the consciousness of his quest as an act of participation in the comprehending story. The "story" thus emerges as the symbolism that will express the awareness of the divine-human movement and countermovement in the quest for truth. One of the profoundest connoisseurs and practitioners of story-telling in the twentieth century, Thomas Mann, has symbolized the divine-human metalepsis of the story in the concluding sentence of his Joseph novel: "And thus ends the beautiful story and God-invention of Joseph and his brothers." Telling a story in this metaleptic sense of the term is not a matter of choice. The story is the symbolic form the questioner has to adopt necessarily when he gives an account of his quest as the event of wresting, by the response of his human search to a divine movement, the truth of reality from a reality pregnant with truth yet unrevealed. Moreover, the story remains the constant symbolism of the quest even when the tension between divine and human story is reduced to the zero of identity as in the dialectical story told by the self-identical *logos* of the Hegelian system.

From the consciousness of the quest as an event whose story must be told as part of the story of reality becoming luminous for its truth, there result a considerable number of problems to be dealt with in later chapters of this volume. For the present we have to concentrate on the implications for the problem of the Beginning.

The great quests for truth in which the consciousness of the metaleptic story becomes differentiated—be they the priestly quest of Genesis with the prophetic quests in the background, or the Judaeo-Christian quest, or the Zoroastrian, the Hinduist and Buddhist, the Confucian and Taoist quests, or finally the noetic quests of the Hellenic philosophers—do not occur in a vacuum. They occur in social fields, constituted by older experiences of order and symbolizations of their truth, now experienced by the questioners to have fallen into disorder and decline. The quest for truth is a movement of resistance to the prevalent disorder; it is an effort to attune the concretely disordered existence again to the truth of the It-reality, an attempt to create a new social field of existential order in competition with the fields whose claim to truth has become doubtful. If the quest succeeds in finding the symbols that will adequately express the newly differentiated experience of order, if it then finds adherents to the new truth and durable forms for their organization, it can indeed become the beginning of a new social field. The account of these personal and social events, however, does not exhaust the story to be told; in addition, the successful establishment of a field of differentiated order creates new structures in history through its relations to other social fields. For the quest, if successful, imposes on the older fields the previously not existent characteristics of falsehood or lie; this imposition will provoke movements of resistance from the adherents to the older, more compact truth, as well as from the discoverers of verities alternative to both the old and the new truth; it will furthermore meet with the social obstacles of spiritual dullness and indifference; and it will encounter movements of skepticism aroused by the new plurality of verities. The quest, thus, is not only its own beginning. By restructuring the social fields at large in their relation to the truth of order, it marks the beginning of a new configuration of truth in history. Since the questioner's quest is accompanied by his consciousness of the event as a beginning in the personal, social, and historical dimensions of order, the questioner has to tell quite a story indeed. It is the story of his experience of disorder, of the resistance aroused in him by the observation of concrete cases, of his experience of being drawn into the search of true order by a command issuing from the It-reality, of his consciousness of ignorance and questioning, of his discovery of the truth, and of the consequences of disorder unrestrained by regard for the order he has experienced and articulated. The event as a beginning is the story of an attempt to impose order on a wasteland of disorder.

The story of the quest is the word that evokes order from disorder by the force of its truth. But how does the listener recognize the story to be true, so that by the recognition of its truth he is forced to reorder his existence? Why should he believe the story to be true rather than consider it somebody's private opinion concerning the order of his preference? To questions of this class only one answer is possible: If the story is to evoke authoritatively the order of a social field, the word must be spoken with an authority recognizable as such by the men to whom the appeal is addressed; the appeal will have no authority of truth unless it speaks with an authority commonly present in everybody's consciousness, however inarticulate, deformed, or suppressed the consciousness in the concrete case may be. Using the Heraclitian distinction of private and public, we may say, the appeal will be no more than a private (*idios*) opinion unless the questioner finds in the course of his quest the word (*logos*) that indeed speaks what is common (*xynon*) to the order of man's existence as a partner in the comprehending reality; only if the questioner speaks the common *logos* of reality can he evoke a truly public order. Or, in the language of Genesis, the story of the quest will have the authority of truth only if it is attuned to a comprehending reality that itself is a story of pneumatic evocation of order from disorder.

The character of truth, thus, attaches to the story by virtue of its paradoxic structure of being both a narrative and an event:

(1) As a narrative, the story of the quest conveys insights into the order of reality by language in the mode of intentionality. The human narrative refers to reality intended in the mode of thing-ness.

(2) As an event, the story emerges from the It-reality; its language articulates an experience in the metaxy of divine-human

movements and countermovements. The story is an event in which the It-reality becomes luminous for its truth. Under the aspect of this second structure the language of the story is not narratively referential but luminously symbolic.

However, although these structures in the story can be distinguished, they must not be hypostatically separated. The story that opens with Genesis 1 must not be construed hypostatically as a narrative told either by a revelatory God or by an intelligently imaginative human being. It is both, because it is neither the one nor the other; and it has this paradoxic character inasmuch as it is not a plain narration of things, but at the same time a symbolism in which the human beginning of order becomes translucent for its meaning as an act of participation in the divine Beginning. The participatory structure of the event and the account given of it in the referential structure of the narrative are inseparably one in the paradoxic structure of the story.

§6. The Story Begins in the Middle

The beginning we have been trying to find is found at last, but we have not come to an end of the story by finding it. For the story of the quest can be a true story only if the questioner participates existentially in the comprehending story told by the It through its creative epiphany of structure. Colloquially expressed: The story cannot begin unless it starts in the middle. Moreover, this paradox applies not only to the story of Genesis, chosen as an exemplar in our analysis, but to our own analysis as well. For in its course, the complex of consciousness-reality, with its paradoxic constitution of intentionality-luminosity, which first appeared in the mode of a thing-reality to be explored, had to be enlarged step by step until the analysis itself became part of the paradoxic complex. It had to be enlarged, first, by including a language that is both conceptual and symbolic; the complex then grew by expanding to a truth dependent for its validity on the participatory quest for truth; it further expanded when the symbolism of the story imposed itself, and the story, finally, moved to the symbolism of a beginning that starts in the middle. As the analysis proceeded, the complex grew without losing its paradoxic character; far from ending as a thing sufficiently analyzed, it drew the analysis into its orbit. The analysis itself is paradoxic in structure.

The large field of implications connected with an analysis that is paradoxic in structure will occupy us later. But the implications emerging more immediately from a beginning that begins in the middle belong to the present context. It will be expedient to unfold the more important issues by starting from their formulation in terms of Plato's experience and symbolization of the metaxy:

(1) The story of the quest, as the account of a participatory event, originates and moves neither in the temporal dimension of external objects nor in the dimension of an eternity, of a divine time out of time, but somewhere in the in-between of the two, i.e., in the dimension symbolized by Plato as the metaxy. From this factor in the paradox there opens the view on the problems of the various modes of time. The factor is one of the experiential reasons that moved Plato to symbolize time as the moving *eikon* of eternity.

(2) The tension between time and eternity, however, must not be transformed into an autonomous object of philosophic discourse, for that would fragmentize the paradoxic complex by hypostatizing the participatory tension to the neglect of the participants at the poles of the tension. With a view to the participants one would have to say on the contrary: The story of the quest is a true beginning of order in external time because it symbolizes the questioner's experience of being drawn toward order by the divine reality out of time; the quest is an eruption of order within time in response to an irruption of order from the beyond of time.

(3) As the one or the other of the factors in the complex is accentuated, the story then does begin in time or it does not begin in time, and the two contradictory statements are both equally true when understood as implications of the complex. The paradox of the true contradictions has its roots in the paradox of a language that speaks in the mode of thing-reality of things that are not things in the sense of external objects; and the paradox of language is part of the paradox of an It-reality becoming luminous for its truth through a consciousness that is located physically in the body of man while it is existentially located in the comprehending metaxy.

(4) Couching the paradox of a story that begins in the middle in terms of the Platonic metaxy, however, cannot be the last word in the matter; if it were, we would not have to engage in a quest of our own but could simply reprint Plato's dialogues; the mere fact that we refer to the Platonic analysis in the context of our own forcefully suggests that the problems surrounding the "middle" are

not exhausted by the symbolism of the metaxy. If the validity of the story depends on its beginning in the middle, then our own story, in order to be valid, must have its beginning in the middle, too; and the middle in which we begin as Western philosophers toward the end of the twentieth century A.D. is not the middle in which the authors of Genesis had to begin their story about 500 B.C.; nor is it the middle in which Plato developed his symbolism. In the pursuit of our questioning, thus, we encounter a plurality of middles, validating a plurality of quests, telling a plurality of stories, all having valid beginnings.

§7. The Plurality of Middles

The plurality of middles, engendering a plurality of true stories, has been observed as a phenomenon as far back as our written records go, to the third millennium B.C. And as far back as the observation itself, there reaches the manifold of variegated responses to it—ranging in conventional patterns from tolerance to intolerance, from questioning doubt to dull indifference, from imperial claims for this story as the one and only truth to diplomatic acceptance of co-existence among a plurality of verities, from pragmatic skepticism that will conform to the dominant truth because peaceful order is preferable to the violent disruption of society by fanatical truth-fighters, through historical relativisms that consider the ever-increasing plurality of middles as conclusive proof that the quest for truth is vain, to the extremes of radical nihilism. These conventional responses, however, although confirming by their millennial recurrence the truth of the observation, contribute little to the analytical understanding of the plurality of middles as a structure in reality. We now have to formulate the issue in continuity with our earlier reflections on the symbolism of the story.

If the story of the quest depends for its truth on being an event in the comprehending reality, a plurality of middles can mean either (1) a plurality of comprehending realities with a corresponding plurality of middles, or (2) a plurality of episodes occurring in the same comprehending It-story. The first possibility must be dismissed as senseless, because we have no experience of a comprehending reality other than its comprehensiveness in relation to reality in its mode of thing-ness. The phantasy of multiple It-realities would transform the It into one of the things comprehended and require a further comprehending reality; the phantasy would abandon the analysis of consciousness, with its structures of intentionality and luminosity, and with the exegetic analysis its experiential basis. If, then, the second possibility is to be accepted, we must accept the reality of an It-story that tells itself through the events of the participatory quests for truth and, with its reality, the implications of the paradoxic symbolism.

The questioner, when he renders the account of his participatory quest, is conscious of a Beginning beyond the beginning and of an End beyond the end of his story. But where do we find the experiential basis for this consciousness of a capitalized Beginning and End beyond the temporal beginning and end of the quest? The question must be raised, because the "beyond" in the preceding sentence obviously is not a spatial preposition adding a stretch of external time to the past and future of the time in which the story is told, but rather a symbol expressing the participation of the temporal story in the dimension of the It-reality out-of-time. If this is the case, however, how does the questioner experience a Beginning and an End that, wherever they lie, certainly do not lie within his present experience? The problem was explored by Plato in the Hellenic context of experience, and he discovered the enigmatic present consciousness that will validate the language of a Beginning and an End in the very structure of the quest itself. Moreover, in the linguistic exegesis of the experienced structure he developed the prepositional "beyond" into the symbol of the divine-immortal Beyond, the *epekeina* of all being things (*ta onta*), including the gods. The presence of the divine Beyond, of the formative *Nous*, is experienced as the formative force in the philosopher's quest for truth. Precisely because this divine Beyond, "this God" as it is called in the *Laws*, is not one of the being things, it is, then, experienced as present in all of them (*pareinai*) as their creatively formative force. The Beyond is not a thing beyond the things, but the experienced presence, the Parousia, of the formative It-reality in all things. The Parousia of the Beyond, experienced in the present of the quest, thus, imposes on the dimension of external time, with its past, present, and future, the dimension of divine presence. The past is not simply in the past, nor the future simply in the future, for both past and future participate in the presence of the same divine-immortal Beyond that is experienced in the present of the questioner's participatory meditation. We have to speak, therefore, of a flux of presence endowing all the phases—past, present, and future—of external time with the structural dimension of an indelible present. The flux of presence is the experienced Parousia of the Beyond in time, the mode of time in which the It tells its tale through the events of the metaleptic quest by endowing it with the indelible present; it is the time of the It-tale that demands expression through the capitalized Beginning and End when the presence of the Beyond is to be symbolized in the questioner's account of his quest.

The metaxy, thus, remains the symbol that validly expresses the experience of existence in the Between of thing-reality, including the bodily location of consciousness, and of Beyond-reality, but certain ramifications of its meaning are discovered when the Beyond becomes more clearly differentiated. These ramifications extend to all the parts of the complex consciousness-reality-language. Above all, the Beyond is understood not to be a thing among things, but is experienced only in its formative presence, in its Parousia. In relation to the immortal-divine Beyond even the formerly immortal gods now become things deriving their immortality from their contemplation of the truly immortal reality of the divine Beyond. We witness the beginnings of an understanding of the "gods" as a language expressing the experience of divine presence in a more compact mode, as well as an awareness that the "intermediate immortality" of the gods does not dissolve into nothingness when the gods are discovered as a compact language in relation to the differentiated language of the Beyond. Moreover, when the Beyond is fully understood as a non-thing, the being things other than the gods can be fully understood in their thingness. They acquire a "nature," this nature understood as the form they have received as their own through the formative presence of the Beyond. However, this nature of the things, this *rerum natura*, can then become, regarding its comparatively stable characteristics, an autonomous matter of exploration, so autonomous indeed that its origin in the formative presence of the Beyond can be forgotten and a capitalized Nature will assume the functions of the It-reality. These various ramifications, and their millennial consequences, will occupy us in later chapters on the Platonic and Christian Parousia, and on the transformations of the symbol Nature. For the present, we have to concentrate on the problems arising more immediately for the structure of the quest for truth.

§8. Definite Thingness and Indefinite Diversification

The distinction between things and a Beyond that endows them with their definite forms loses such clarity as it has when we move from external objects (artifacts and organisms are the exemplars of things favored by Aristotle) to the existential area of reality in which the symbols of things and their forms have their origin, i.e., to the experiential complex that becomes articulate in the symbolism of consciousness-reality-language. This complex of experience and symbolization represents a kind of things whose structures are recognizable but do not have the character of definite forms of things with a beginning and an end in time. We encounter a type of diversification that is not the same as the definite, and definable, relation between genus and species, or between a species and the individuals subsumed, but rather that of a form in process of formation, or failure of formation, with a Beginning and an End out of time. We had to note the peculiar diversification of the complex through the modes of compactness and differentiation; the diversification of compactness through the language of the myth, through mythospeculative constructions of the cosmogonic type, and through pneumatically differentiated mythospeculations; the further diversification of differentiated types of consciousness through the experiential accents on either the divine irruption of the *pneuma* or on the noetic quest in response to a divine movement; the diversification of these various types in a plurality of ethnic cultures; within the ethnic cultures, the diversification through personalities and social fields; and as a result of the personal and social diversifications, the creation of diversified historical fields of truth. And yet, this indefinitely diversified field, with its plurality of beginnings and ends, is definitely recognizable as a field of languages, intelligibly symbolizing the truth of reality in conformity with the recognizable structure of the complex.

Even more, within the field of indefinite diversification there can be discerned definite lines of meaning, such as the lines of advancing knowledge regarding the world of things and advancing clarity regarding the It-reality, not the least important of these lines becoming manifest in the symbolism that allows us to distinguish between things and the Beyond of things. The lines of meaning, furthermore, do not occur as facts blind to themselves, to be discovered as such only by later generations in retrospect, but as events accompanied by the consciousness of an advance that, at the same time, is the consciousness of a previous quest falling short of the advance. As a consequence, both quests move into a reflective distance in relation to a consciousness that becomes the source of criteria by which the truth of the quest is to be judged. And finally, the criteria really emerge from the history of the quest as the quest becomes reflectively intelligible for its own structure in the existential experiences symbolized by the complex consciousness-reality-language. The present analysis thus confirms the statement by which this study on *Order and History* opened, the statement: "The order of history emerges from the history of order."

But what does "emerge" mean? do we step out of the process of the quest after all and arrive at results in terms of intentionalist concepts? will there emerge a truth at last that has the character of a generalization or abstraction from a multitude of individual cases?

§9. Formative Parousia and Deformation

The questions touch a cardinal problem inherent to the analysis of existential consciousness, the inherent temptation that is every questioner's burden, the temptation to deform the Beyond and its formative Parousia, as they are experienced and symbolized in the respective quest, by transforming the Beyond into a thing and its Parousia into the imposition of a definite form on reality. The temptation not only affects the present analysis, but is a constant force in the millennial process of the quest for truth. I shall recall some of its manifestations that have become topical in earlier contexts. There are the mythospeculative, imperial constructions of a one-line history that is envisaged as reaching its divine End in the present end of the speculator's story; this is the type that extends from the Sumerian king-list to Hegel's imperial speculation. When the divine Beyond, then, becomes inchoatively differentiated by the Israelite prophets, an Isaiah can indulge in the magic phantasy of forcing the End of the It-story on the end of a war with Assyria by a royal act of faith that will transfigure the pragmatic conditions of warfare into the final victory of the It-reality; this type of metastatic speculation, as I have called it, again has remained a constant into the metastatic faith-movements of the twentieth century A.D. When the transfiguration through a royal act of faith does not occur and the political disasters reach insurmountability, the metastatic type of speculation then gives way to the apocalyptic type, which expects disorder of catastrophic magnitude to be ended by divine intervention. And when the divine intervention does not occur, the apocalyptic is paralleled and followed by the gnostic type, which construes the genesis of the cosmos with its catastrophes of ecumenic-imperial domination as the consequence of a psychodramatic fall in the Beyond, now to be reversed by the gnostics' action on the basis of their pneumatic understanding (gnosis) of the drama. The Beginning was a mistake to begin with and the end of the gnostic story will bring it to its End.

The story of the symbolisms engendered by disturbances of existential consciousness has a fascination of its own, but we must not let its charm obscure its deformative character, or the correlation between structures deformed and the structure of the deformation. The cosmos does not disappear just because there are gnostic dreamers around; their dreams are events within the cosmos they wish to abolish; and we still have to live in the cosmos when the various apocalyptic and gnostic sectarian movements have run their respective courses. If placed in the context of reality experienced, the recall of the cases will illuminate the tension between conceptually definite and indefinitely diversified structures that is our present concern.

The symbols enumerated can be read as a list of individual cases to be subsumed under the general concept of a disturbance of consciousness, perhaps of the *nosos* of the soul in the classic sense; and if one stops thinking at this point they will remain such a list, to be conscientiously reported in a positivistic "history of ideas." If, however, one does not stop thinking, the recall will read as a "story" of deformative symbols engendered parallel with the formative differentiation of the Beyond in the Near Eastern ethnic cultures of the cosmological empires and the Chosen People. The recall, far from being a plain account of indifferently equal cases coming under a general head, tells a story of increasingly conscious resistance to beginnings that come to an end without reaching the End, culminating in the phantasy of a beginning that will make an end of the Beginning. In the context of the story, therefore, the cases partake of the diversification that characterizes the quest for truth. Parallel with the diversified history of truth and of attunement to its order, and closely related to its substance, there appears to run a diversified history of untruth and disorder. If we now ask the question whether the recognition of the recall as a "story" makes nonsense of its conception as a list of individual cases of a general type, the answer will have to be: yes and no. The symbols enumerated are indeed individual cases of a general type of deformation, recognizably of the same type that prevails in Hellenic, Hellenistic, Christian, and modern contexts, but at the same time they are in all of these contexts parts of a "story" that runs parallel with the story of the differentiating quest for truth. The intentionalist thingness of the cases is inseparable from a complex of structures that comprehends the diversification of the quest. What "emerges" from the analysis, thus, is neither intentionalist thingness nor diversification, but a complex that comprehends them both. This complex in the recall requires some further reflection.

§10. Existential Resistance

The structures governing the complex will come into view if we consider that the recalling story of the cases reveals a movement of existential resistance to existence in a reality in which the "things," including man and society, come to an end in time without coming to their End out-of-time. The truth of reality is not questioned; it is resisted. We have to distinguish, therefore, between resistance to truth and agreement or disagreement about the optimal symbolization of truth experienced. The resisters are human beings, endowed with the same kind of consciousness as the thinkers who are engaged in the quest for truth; their experience of reality is the same as that of the questioning thinkers; they do not deny that reality has indeed the structure symbolized by the pneumatic and noetic questioners. There should be stressed the frequently overlooked agreement of the deformers with the searchers for truth that reality is not exhausted by thingness in time. The resisters are just as conscious as the prophets and philosophers of the movement in reality beyond its present structure; and they know just as well that reality moves not only into a future of things but toward their Beyond. More recent symbolisms of deformative resistance, such as the "transcendence into the future" (*Transzendenz in die Zukunft*), reveal by their very formulation the distinction they purpose to obscure; nor should there be forgotten the contemporary enmity between certain representatives of "positivism" and ideological activists. Since the resisters do not disagree with the truth they resist, the experientially cardinal issue comes into focus: Why do they resist a truth they neither deny nor can change? and what are the experiential sources that endow resistance with such strength of meaning that it becomes a constant force in history?

The motives of resistance have a surface of obviousness. The resisters are dissatisfied with the want of order they experience in their personal and social existence. Measured by the Solonic "unseen measure," the reality in which they live does all too visibly not conform to the form demanded by the divine ordering force of the Beyond. The story of their existence is not the story the It-reality wants to tell.

At the basis of the experienced dissatisfaction lie the general miseries that afflict human existence, enumerated by Hesiod as hunger, hard work, disease, early death, and the injuries the weaker must suffer at the hands of the stronger. This general potential of dissatisfaction can then be exponentially aggravated by the disturbances of personal and social existence through events with historical mass effect. To the class of these events belong a variety of phenomena. From the demographic side one would have to consider large population movements through migration and conquest, unsettling whether peaceful or violent, unsettling alike for conquerors and conquered; furthermore, sudden decreases of population caused by human epidemics, mass starvation caused by the spread of animal and vegetable pests, and increases of population beyond the subsistence level provided by the economic and technical potential of place and time. From the political-pragmatic side one would have to consider the vast destruction of ethnic cultures by the imperial entrepreneurs of the Ecumenic Age and the subsequent rise of imperial-dogmatic civilizations from the wreckage of the ecumenic empires. For the modern period one would have to add the creation of the power differential between the Western and all other civilizations through the intellectual, scientific, commercial, and industrial revolutions in the West, as well as the exploitation of the differential to the global limits; the decline of Western power and order through the internal conflicts caused by the rise of imperial nationalisms and of equally imperial ideological movements; and the resistance of the non-Western civilizational societies to the destruction of their own cultures by a Western global ecumenism.

In the concrete cases, thus, there is ample reason to be dissatisfied with the order of existence. The resisters are keenly aware of the discrepancy between the disorder they have to suffer and the order they have lost, or which they despair to maintain or judge to lie beyond any probability of ever being gained; they are disappointed with the slowness of the movement in reality toward the order they experience as the true order demanded by the Beyond; they are morally aroused by, and angry with, the misery that the slowness of the transfiguring movement in reality entails; and the experiences of this class can heighten to the conviction that something is fundamentally wrong with reality itself, if it always bungles the movement toward the order supposed to be its meaning. At this point, when the resistance to disorder transforms itself into a revolt against the very process of reality and its structure, the tension of formative existence in the divine-human movement and countermovement of the metaxy can break down; the presence of the Beyond, its Parousia, is no longer experienced as an effective ordering force, and, as a consequence, the questioner for truth can no longer tell a story that is part of the story told by the It-reality. At the extreme of the revolt in consciousness, "reality" and the "Beyond" become two separate entities, two "things," to be magically manipulated by suffering man for the purpose of either abolishing "reality" altogether and escaping into the "Beyond," or of forcing the order of the "Beyond" into "reality." The first of the magic alternatives is preferred by the Gnostics of antiquity, the second one by the modern gnostic thinkers.

§11. Imagination

The analysis, while pursuing the surface motives of the resisters to the extreme of their expression in magic operations, could not be conducted without constantly touching on the deeper stratum of resistance, i.e., on its source in the structure of questioning consciousness itself. In the depth of the quest, formative truth and deformative untruth are more closely related than the language of "truth" and "resistance" would suggest. For "truth" is not, as the surface language suggests, a something lying around to be accepted, rejected, or resisted; imagining "truth" as a thing would deform the structure of consciousness in the same manner as does the transformation of the symbols "reality" and "Beyond" into things for the purpose of manipulation. Truth has its reality in the symbols engendered by the quest, and the quest has its reality in the metaxy of divine-human movements and countermovements. The symbols, thus, arise from the human response to the appeal of reality, and the response is burdened with its character as an event in the reality to which it responds.

At this point it will be helpful to introduce the term "imagination" into the analysis. The event, we may say, is imaginative in the sense that man can find the way from his participatory experience of reality to its expression through symbols.

If, however, we use the term "imagination," sanctioned by its usage in the philosophers' language since antiquity, to denote this ability to find the way from the metaleptic experiences to the imagery of expressive symbols, the paradoxic structure of the complex of consciousness-reality-language compels us to raise certain questions concerning object and subject of imagination. If the symbols imagined express the experience of reality, will they express reality experienced by man as a something, or will they express the experience as an event in the comprehending reality? And is imagination, as to its subject, a "faculty" of man to create symbols? Or would we not rather have to say that the existence of a way from metaleptic experience to symbolization reveals reality as internally imaginative and, inasmuch as the symbols are meant to be "true," as internally cognitive, so that the comprehending reality, rather than man, would become the subject endowed with imagination? In keeping with our analysis, neither of the alternatives posed by the questions can be affirmed to the exclusion of the other one; the paradox of consciousness governs imagination, too. Imagination, as a structure in the process of a reality that moves toward its truth, belongs both to human consciousness in its bodily location and to the reality that comprehends bodily located man as a partner in the community of being. There is no truth symbolized without man's imaginative power to find the symbols that will express his response to the appeal of reality; but there is no truth to be symbolized without the comprehending It-reality in which such structures as man with his participatory consciousness, experiences of appeal and response, language, and imagination occur. Through the imaginative power of man the It-reality moves imaginatively toward its truth.

Nevertheless, governed as it is by the paradoxic structure of the complex of consciousness-reality, imagination offers imagining man escapes of a sort from the reality by which it is governed. The diversified variety of these escapes is by now sufficiently familiar not to require elaboration. We can concentrate on the source of the escapes in the tension between imaginative force and the reality in which it occurs, between the image of reality and the reality it is supposed to image.

By virtue of his imaginative responsiveness man is a creative partner in the movement of reality toward its truth; and this creatively formative force is exposed to deformative perversion, if the creative partner imagines himself to be the sole creator of truth. The imaginative expansion of participatory into sole power makes possible the dream of gaining ultimate power over reality through the power of creating its image. The distance inherent in the metaleptic tension can be obscured by letting the reality that reveals itself in imaginative truth imaginatively dissolve into a truth that reveals reality. We are touching the potential of deformation that has been discerned, ever since antiquity, as a human vice under such symbols as hybris, pleonexia, *alazoneia tou biou, superbia vitae,* pride of life, *libido dominandi,* and will to power. In the Romantic period, the vice has found its most impressive characterization in the "statement" of the Baccalaureus in *Faust:* "The world, it was not before I created it." The image of the world becomes the world itself. By his imagination, we may say, man can out-imagine himself and out-comprehend the comprehending reality.

The imaginative perversion of participatory imagination into an autonomously creative power has remained a constant in history however well its manifestations have been observed, described, diagnosed, criticized, dramatized, disapproved, anathematized, ironized, ridiculed, and satirized. And as far as we can discern analytically, it will not disappear in the future. For imaginative perversion is not a mistake in a syllogism or a system, to be thrown out for good once it is discovered, but a potential in the paradoxic play of forces in reality as it moves toward its truth. The movement toward truth always resists an untruth. Every thinker who is engaged in the quest for truth resists a received symbolism he considers insufficient to express truly the reality of his responsive experience. In order to aim at a truer truth he has to out-imagine the symbols hitherto imagined; and in the assertion of his imaginative power he can forget that he is out-imagining symbols of truth, but not the process of reality in which he moves as a partner. The resister, inversely, although he may be dominated by his *libido dominandi* to the point of grotesquely imagining himself the creator of a world in ultimate truth, need not at all be wrong in perceiving the insufficiencies of order and symbolization that arouse his wrath. The thinker engaged in the formative quest is a human being plagued by the forces of self-assertive resistance in his soul just as much as his counterpart, the resister to the paradoxic structure of consciousness-reality, is plagued by the truth of reality. As a consequence, a movement of resistance, if it achieves clarity about its experiential motivations and elaborates the story of its deformative quest, can contribute substantially to the understanding of the paradox in the formative structure it resists, while the defenders of the truth may fall into the various traps prepared by their own self-assertive resistance and thus contribute substantially to an understanding of the forces of deformation.

§12. The Symbols Reflective Distance-Remembrance-Oblivion

The analysis has traced the resistance to truth to the ground it has in common with the resistance to untruth, to its ground in the assertive imagination of man as a force in reality. The power of imagination, however, while assertive of truth, is not necessarily self-assertive. The thinker engaged in the quest for truth can remain, or become, aware of the structure of his quest. He can be conscious of his state of ignorance concerning true order and be aware that a consciousness of ignorance presupposes the apprehension of something knowable beyond his present state of knowledge; he can experience himself as surrounded by a horizon of knowable truth toward which he can move, even if he does not reach it; he can feel himself drawn to move, and he can sense that he is moving in the right direction when he moves toward the Beyond of the horizon that creates the horizon; in brief, he can be conscious of his participatory role in the process of experience, imagination, and symbolization. He can discover the dimension of consciousness that has been implied, and frequently referred to, in the present analysis, but not yet made explicitly thematic:

the reflective distance of consciousness to its own participation in thing-reality and It-reality. The thinker may be tempted, but he is not forced, to heighten his assertive participation in the imaginative symbolization of truth to a self-assertive, autonomous ultimacy; he need not deform the beginning of his quest into a Beginning that brings the End of all beginnings. He can remember his experience of movements and countermovements in the metaxy as the reality from which his assertive insights into true order have emerged, and he can express his remembrance through such reflective symbols as the tension of the metaxy, the poles of the tension, the things and their Beyond, thing-reality and It-reality, the human and the divine, intentionality and luminosity, the paradox of consciousness-reality-language, and the complex of participation-assertion-self-assertion.

The symbols enumerated have occurred frequently in the present analysis and have caused us, on occasion, to raise the question whether they are concepts intending a thing-reality, or symbols expressing the It-reality, or no more than pieces of empty talk—questions that had to remain in suspense at the time. We are listing the symbols now as manifestations of a consciousness that is structured not only by the paradox of intentionality and luminosity, but also by an awareness of the paradox, by a dimension to be characterized as a reflectively distancing remembrance. It is the dimension that Plato has symbolized expressively, although still rather compactly, as the noetic *anamnesis*. This third dimension of consciousness, however, does not function automatically as a formative force in the existential quest for truth. The thinker, it is true, cannot abolish the reflective distance of his consciousness to its own existential structure, but in his remembrance he can imaginatively forget this or that part of the paradoxically complex event; and when a thinker, whatever his motives may be, forgets his role as a partner in being, and with this role the metaleptic character of his quest, he can deform the remembered assertive power of imagination in his quest imaginatively into the sole power of truth. Imaginative remembrance of the process, the remembrance intended by Plato, implies the potential of imaginative oblivion.

The terms used in the preceding paragraph to express the experience of reflective distance in consciousness are new. They draw for their validity on the context of the anamnetic meditation as the event from which they imaginatively emerge. In our time, however, that is not enough to make their validity convincing. They are exposed to the conventional misunderstandings resulting from the deformation of meditative statements into propositions about things, from the fragmentation of experiential and symbolic complexes into their parts, and the hypostatization of the parts into definitional concepts referring to definable things. A few elaborative remarks will, therefore, be in order.

1. Their Validity in the Context of the Meditation

The first issue is the contextual validity of the symbols as they emerge from the anamnetic meditation. There is no imaginative oblivion without remembrance. The something forgotten in the act of oblivion is not an external object mislaid, or overlooked, or inaccessible at the time of the act, but the inescapably present structure of existence, symbolized by the complex of consciousness-reality, of thing-reality and It-reality, of the things and their Beyond. An imaginative resister may be even more acutely aware of the existential reality he resists than a complacent believer and conformer, as Saint Augustine on occasion observed; he may remember too well what he wants to forget. There is, furthermore, no remembrance or oblivion without the reflective distance to the experienced paradox of existence; nor is there anything to be forgotten or remembered without the existential consciousness to which the acts in reflective distance pertain. And finally, there is no existential consciousness without the reality in which it is conscious of occurring, this reality extending to the embodiment of consciousness in man, to the thing-reality surrounding the thingness of the human body, and to the It-reality with its divinely formative force. The analysis, thus, is a coherent whole engendering a coherent complex of symbols that endows the single symbols with their contextual validity. Hence, the single symbols must not be deformed by being imagined to be concepts referring to "things"; the whole must not be fragmented into entities independent of the whole—a game of "ontological" specialization that has become socially dominant ever since the invention of "ontology" in the seventeenth century. This does not mean, however, that the analysis as a whole is beyond criticism: Substantive errors, if they have occurred, must be exposed and corrected. Nor does it mean that the "whole" of the analysis is exhaustive: At every point it can be expanded into further details. Nor is the analysis, even if it should prove tenable on its principal points, the last word in the matter it explores: Its course is determined by its beginning from the symbolism of Beginning. It will have to be supplemented by analytical explorations starting from other points in the structure of consciousness, as for instance from the experiences and symbolizations of the Beyond or the End, or from the Visions of a Whole of reality. Such supplemental meditations will lead to insights that have not come to attention in the present analysis.

2. Their Validity in the Context of Historical Equivalences

The second issue is the validity of the symbols in the context of their historical equivalences. The symbols are new, but the experience in need of differentiating analysis is not; in fact, the effort to cope with the variety of its aspects is a millennial constant in the process of the quest for truth. For the present purpose we need not go further back than to Plato's exegesis of the complex remembrance-oblivion. His analysis is "noetic" in the specific, still rather compact sense of a meditation dominated by the symbolism of the *Nous* as the "third god," after Kronos and Zeus, who will now, in the new historical situation, form the order of existence by his presence, his Parousia, in the participatory consciousness of man; we are at the juncture where noetic analysis proper begins to differentiate from the compact mythic experience and symbolization of reality. In this transitional situation, Plato expresses the experience of oblivion by the symbol *anoia*, conventionally translated as "folly," which lets the accent fall on the resister's disorder of existence rather than on the acts of imaginative oblivion caused by it. The resister guilty of *anoia* is a man who does not remember his role as a partner in the community of being, who has managed to make himself unconscious of his consciousness of questing participation in the divine Beyond, in the *Nous,* and who as a consequence can transform his assertive participation into self-assertion. The man who resists his formation through the divine *Nous* deforms himself; he becomes a fool.

The symbol *anoia*, however, has not survived in philosophical discourse; even worse, because of its compactness, it has become practically untranslatable into a modern language. If *Nous* be translated as reason, its negation would have to become un-reason, if the association of the symbolism *nous-anoia* is to be preserved. Such usage, however, would be linguistically infelicitous because the symbol "reason" has undergone, since the time of Plato, substantial changes of meaning through the movements of Christian theology and of Enlightenment rationalism. Christian theology has denatured the Platonic *Nous* by degrading it imaginatively to a "natural reason," a source of truth subsidiary to the overriding source of revelation; by an act of imaginative oblivion the revelatory tension in Plato's vision of the Nous as the "third god" was eclipsed, in order to gain for the Church a monopoly on revelation. But history has taken its revenge. The nonrevelatory reason, imagined by the theologians as a servant, has become a self-assertive master. In historical sequence, the imagined nonrevelatory reason has become the real antirevelatory reason of the Enlightenment revolt against the Church. The resistance to the social power of intellectually inert, self-assertive institutions has motivated the acts of imaginative oblivion that eclipse the noetic-revelatory truth preserved in ecclesiastical doctrines that have become inflexible. Moreover, since Enlightened resisters can no more than anybody else escape the structure of consciousness, they had to arrogate the authority of noetic truth for their resistance to it; in the form of the various ideologies, resistance to noetic truth, understanding itself as resistance to "irrationality," has become the ultimately legitimizing source of truth revealed. The usurped monopoly of revelation has migrated from the ecclesiastic institutions to their ideological successor establishments, down to the revelatory "statements" through acts of violent destruction in the contemporary movements of terrorism.

3. Reflective Distance

The third issue is the dimension of reflective distance itself, with its potential of both remembrance and oblivion. Its differentiated meaning will have become clear from the course of the present analysis as a third dimension of consciousness. The structure of consciousness, symbolized by the complex of consciousness-reality-language and the paradox of intentionality and luminosity, of thing-reality and It-reality, is not simply "there" as the structure of a finite object to be occasionally discovered. It is not a "thing" to be described or not, but has its reflective presence in consciousness itself. Whatever the mode of consciousness may be in the plurality of its diversification, whether it appears on the scale of compactness and differentiation, or of formation and deformation, it is reflectively present to itself in its symbolization. Moreover, the reflective presence is not confined to the single instances of consciousness as closed entities. As we have seen, the plurality of diversified instances was observed and the observation induced reflective responses; and the events of differentiation were not simply present in reflective consciousness, but were accompanied by reflection on the phenomenon of differentiation and on the new configurations of truth in history created by it. Whatever the order of history may ultimately be, there is a history of order because the truth of consciousness is documenting itself as a historical process through the reflectiveness of symbolizing consciousness. The history of consciousness, as I formulated it, is internally cognitive.

Digression on Rescue of Symbols

Imaginative oblivion deforms consciousness. The confusion of language in the wake of the millennial movements is the syndrome of a disorder that has grown in contemporary Western society to the proportions of an established, in the sense of publicly accepted, state of unconsciousness—not to forget the global extension of the disorder through the power dynamics of Western ecumenism. If we want to break out of the public unconscious, we must analyze it and thereby raise it into consciousness: We must remember the historical acts of oblivion; in order to identify them as acts of oblivion, then, we must remember the paradoxic complex of consciousness-reality-language as the criterion of remembrance and oblivion; and in order to recognize the paradoxic complex as the criterion of truth and untruth, we must differentiate the dimension of reflective distance that stands, compactly implied in the Platonic *anamnesis,* at the beginning of all noetic philosophizing. Only when the complex of reflective distance-remembrance-oblivion is sufficiently differentiated and articulated will it be possible to rescue the symbols that have been historically developed to describe the phenomena of oblivion from their historiographic burial as "ideas," "opinions," or "beliefs," to decide which of them can still be used in the present, confused situation, and to restore them to their legitimate function in the noetic context.

A few reminders and suggestions:

(1) The term *"anoia"* should be restored to usage because it most clearly expresses the state of oblivion as a deformation of noetic consciousness. The translation as "un-reason" or "irrationality" is at present unusable for the reasons given earlier. The translation as "folly," preferred by the classicists, is correct but loses the relation to *Nous.* It has the further disadvantage of conflicting with the "folly" by which the King James Version translates the Hebrew *nabala,* the "foolishness" of denying the existence of God, with its accent on the pneumatic constitution of consciousness. The Greek and Latin translations of *nabala* as *moria* and *insipientia* do not suggest usable English versions either. But one should note that in his compact usage Plato lets *anoia* cover the pneumatic *nabala,* too.

(2) The terms "disorder" or "disturbance" of consciousness that I frequently use translate the *nosos* or *nosema* of Aeschylus and Plato, as well as the *morbus animi,* the "disease of the mind" of Cicero. Plato's medical language becomes quite poignant when he warns of noetic morbidity. In *Gorgias* 480 he speaks of the *nosema tes adikias,* the "disease of injustice," which, if not cured in time, can become an incurable cancer of the soul (*hypoulon kai aniaton*). In *Laws* 716 a man can let his soul become inflamed (*phlegetai*) to a state of self-assertive inflation (*exartheis*) by arrogance, by pride in wealth or social status, or in comeliness of body, or by youthful fervor, a state in which he believes himself to be no longer in need of guidance but able to guide others and as a result brings ruin on himself and society. In such passages one can sense Plato groping for the language that will make well-observed phenomena of personal and social disorder intelligible as a disease of noetic consciousness.

(3) Three hundred years later, after the upheavals of Alexander's conquest, of the Diadochic empires, and of the Roman imperial expansion, the noetic morbidity of the situation seems to have become a much discussed matter-of-course. In his *Tusculan Disputations* (IV, 23–32) a Cicero can speak flatly of the *morbus animi,* identify it as an *aspernatio rationis,* a "rejection of reason," and discuss the symptoms of the disease. Among its variegated manifestations he mentions restless moneymaking, status-seeking, womanizing, overeating, addiction to delicacies and snacks, wine-tippling, irascibility, anxiety, desire for fame and public recognition, rigidity of attitude, and such fears of contact with other human beings as misogyny and misanthropy. The list is timeless enough

to be modern as well, although one could add a few items such as drug addiction, much discussed by Plato in the two forms of addiction to chemicals and addiction to sophistic constructs of untruth, or the spreading of pornography and modern ideologies, well demonstrated in their intimate connection by the Marquis de Sade in his *Philosophie dans le boudoir.*

(4) Although the Ciceronian conception of the *morbus* and its symptoms deserve to become food for thought among psychiatrists who operate with immanentist models of the psyche and of human conduct, it must not be accepted uncritically. That would mean ignoring the formidable difficulties of the Stoic psychology of Pathos and Logos in the background, as well as the satirical observations of Horace on the Stoic results. Still, the language of "disease" and "disorder" has its solid foundation in the existential exegesis of the Hellenic tragedians and historians who experienced the personal and social disorder of their time as a disturbance of consciousness, and of Plato who conceived his philosophizing as a therapeutic persuasion, as a salvational effort to heal the pneumatic and noetic disorder of the psyche. We cannot dispense with it, provided the *aspernatio rationis* be understood to refer to the acts of imaginative oblivion that I try to differentiate, as well as to their subphenomena.

(5) Our rich contemporary experience of such acts, their subphenomena, and their consequences, appears to exert some pressure to find the language that will express the experience. I frequently use the term "Second Reality," created by Robert Musil and Heimito von Doderer, to denote the imaginative constructs of ideological thinkers who want to eclipse the reality of existential consciousness. Moreover, in his *Daemonen* Doderer has developed the symbol of *Apperzeptionsverweigerung,* of the refusal to apperceive, which comes in its meaning very close to the Ciceronian *aspernatio rationis* in the sense of a deliberate act of imaginative oblivion. In everyday usage I furthermore notice the appearance of such phrases as "selective conscience" and "defensive obtuseness" (whose authors I do not know), referring in polite language to a variety of disorderly phenomena ranging from the intellectual crookedness of political activists, through the semiliteracy of trendy career opportunists and the profounder illiteracy imposed by the educational system, to plain stupidity.

(6) And finally, we must remember Aristotle's "All men by nature desire to know." The sentence is the crystal symbol that opens the

great reflective study of consciousness, the act of remembering its range from sense perception to its participation in the divine *Nous.* It opens the quest for the truth of reality (*tes arches theoria*) as the quest for the *arche tes kinemos* (or Plato's *arche tes geneseos*), for the beginning of genesis as a formative movement. If this sentence were torn out of its noetic context, it could be ridiculed as an empirically false statement; for quite a few men obviously do not desire to know but are engaged in the construction of Second Realities and, obsessed by their defensive obtuseness, refuse to apperceive reality. If, however, we do not literalize the sentence and thereby destroy its noetic validity, it will express a thinker's conscious openness toward the paradox of existential consciousness; and it will furthermore symbolize this openness as the potential of "all men," even though the potential be deformed through acts of oblivion by all too many. Through Henri Bergson's *Deux sources de la morale et de la religion* the symbolism of "openness" and "closure," of *l'âme ouverte* and *l'âme close,* has become an effectively differentiated part of the philosophers' language that will allow us to speak unequivocally of the existential states of remembrance and oblivion.

The survey of symbols, suitable and unsuitable, should be sufficient to elucidate the linguistic confusion under which we labor, as well as the necessity of rescuing such symbols as have been successfully developed from the fate of being sucked under by the indifferently lethal morass of "ideas" and "opinions," restoring them to their noetic status.

2

Reflective Distance *vs.* Reflective Identity

We could be brief on the meaning of the reflective dimension in the context of our own analysis. The symbolism of reflective "distance," however, has been formulated in opposition to, and as a corrective of, the symbolism of reflective "identity" developed by the German idealistic philosophers in their great attempt at differentiating the anamnetic structure of consciousness more adequately in its personal, social, and historical aspects. This corrective meaning of the symbol "distance" in relation to the symbol "identity" requires some further elaboration.

§1. The German Revolution of Consciousness

The purpose of the German thinkers was formative. In order to recover the experiential basis of consciousness, they wanted to remove the layers of proportional incrustations accumulated through the centuries of thinking in the intentionalist subject-object mode. In the eighteenth century the mode had culminated in a new wave of definitional and propositional systematizations of metaphysics, ontology, and theology that had made the intentionalist method of dealing with the structures of consciousness convincingly unconvincing. The deformation of consciousness through "metaphysics" and "ontology" was explicitly the target Hegel attacked by means of his *Wissenschaft der Logik*. The attempt at recovery, however, was severely handicapped by the force of tradition that the habit of thinking in terms of thing-reality had acquired, a tradition that was further fortified at the time by the success of the natural sciences, by the prestige of Newtonian physics, and, of special importance for the German thinkers, by its legitimation as the model of "experience" through Kant's *Critique of Pure Reason*. The ambivalent position and function of the *Critique* in this context should be noted. By clarifying the meaning of spatiotemporal experience, it is true, the *Critique* had left no doubt that there was more to "Reason" than physics; the area of the It-reality had been, if not reestablished, at least brought into view again as the area of "Reason" that could not adequately be expressed through the application of "*natuerliche Erkenntnis*," of thinking in subject-object categories. But precisely the characterization of the subject-object mode as the unquestioned, dominant "*natuerliche Erkenntnis*," as well as the acute feeling that the recovery of the "un-natural" experiential basis of philosophy was a revolution of Copernican proportions, betrays the force of the tradition that had to be overcome. In this situation of philosophical deterioration it is no wonder Kant had difficulties in finding the language that would match his revolutionary effort. In fact, in order to denote the "more" than physics that is to be found in "Reason," he could do no better than to coin the symbol *Ding-an-sich*. Since the internal confusion of the famous symbol is not sufficiently realized even today, as far as I can see, it will not be improper to stress that "in-itself" the thing is not a "thing" but the structure of the It-reality in consciousness. The technical problems engendered by the symbol, however, are not the present concern; rather, the symbol's character as a symptom of the pressures that let the attempt to recover the experiences move existential consciousness into the position of a "thing" must be explored.

The dominance of thing-reality in the symbolizing imagination of the time determined the shape of the problems as they emerged in the process of recovering the structure of consciousness. If the "facts of consciousness," the starting point of Fichte's *Wissenschaftslehre* of 1794, were an object to be explored, there had to be a subject that did the exploring, and if there was a subject it had to have a consciousness reflecting on consciousness. What then was the relation between the consciousness of the subject and the "facts of consciousness" it explored? The problem of the reflective dimension of consciousness had been reduced to the relation between two acts of consciousness. As a solution to this problem, however, the plain construction of a reflective act on the part of the subject would be unsuitable, because under this assumption the act of reflection would become a further "fact of consciousness" to be reflected upon by a further act of a further subject. The purely intentionalist construction would have dissolved the integrality of existential consciousness into an indefinite chain of subjective acts. If the integrality was to be preserved, the intentionalist conditions under which the problem had been formulated would require the identification of the reflecting subject as man's *Ich* with the *Ich* of existential consciousness. This self-identical *Ich* was then imagined to be not a further fact of consciousness but the transcendental form of consciousness, immediately evident in an act, not of "experience," but of "intellectual intuition." Since in this identification of the two *Ichs*, however, the accent of construction had fallen on the reflecting subject, and since the reflective act had been conceived by Reinhold, Fichte's predecessor at Jena, in his *Satz des Bewusstseins*, on the subject-object model, the nonparticipatory intentionalism of the reflective act could usurp the authority of participatory consciousness.[1]

To denote this new type of deformed consciousness the German thinkers developed the symbol "speculation." The historical process of consciousness, with its internally cognitive authority, was abandoned in favor of an externally authoritative "speculation" that would allow the thinker to take his imaginative stand in a reflective-speculative act beyond the process. The tension of existence in the metaxy had been eclipsed; Plato's Beyond of divine reality had become incarnate in the "beyond" of the speculator's imagination. As a consequence, the speculation could proclaim itself as the ultimate revelation of existential consciousness and, in this capacity, as the force that would determine all future history. The history of order had been transformed into an order of history whose truth had been made intelligible through the speculator's effort, and since its truth had become intelligible, it could be brought to its conclusion in reality according to the speculator's System of Science. The reality experienced and symbolized by everyman's conscious existence was to be replaced by the Second Reality of speculation; the historical beginning of the speculative System was to be the true Beginning leading to the true End of history. Questions concerning the structure of the speculator's own consciousness, the questions concerning the truth it embodied in terms of remembrance and

---

1. For a fuller discussion of the Fichte development, see Ulrich Claesges, *Geschichte des Selbstbewusstseins: Der ursprung des spekulativen Problems in Fichtes Wissenschaftslehre von 1794–95* (Den Haag, 1974). The footnotes to the text for *In Search of Order* were prepared by Paul Caringella.

oblivion, were not permitted. This last requirement, necessary to protect the speculative efforts against all-too-obvious questions, was raised to the rank of an explicit postulate by Karl Marx.

The creation of speculative imagination as the new source of truth in history was a revolutionary event indeed. As we know from numerous statements by Reinhold, Fichte, Schelling, Hegel, Friedrich Schlegel, and Schiller, the actors of the event interpreted it as the German variant of the general revolution that was taking place on the pragmatic level in America, France, and the Netherlands (Batavian Republic of 1795). They derived the intensity of their fervor from the sense of participating in a world-historic revolution of consciousness. Moreover, with a nationalist coloration of this fervor the German thinkers were convinced that their own revolution of the "spirit" ranked higher than the parallel pragmatic revolutions because it reached more radically into the depth of consciousness and thus would have, in the long run, the more lasting pragmatic effect. In a letter of October 28, 1808, Hegel wrote to his friend Niethammer that, as every day further convinced him, theoretical work accomplishes more in the world than does practical work—"once the realm of perception [*Vorstellung*] is revolutionized, reality cannot hold out." And one of the most astute observers of the event, Heinrich Heine, in his *History of Religion and Philosophy in Germany*, anticipates that the "revolution in the spirit" will be followed by "the same revolution in the realm of phenomena." Thought, he continues, "precedes deed as lightning precedes thunder"; the thunder will be slow in coming as Germans move cumbersomely and slowly; "but once, when you hear it crash as it never has crashed before in world-history, you will know: the German thunder has arrived."[2]

Although the event is historiographically well known in the minutest detail, its critical analysis still leaves much to be desired. It is so insufficient indeed that we do not even have a commonly accepted term to characterize the event's structure, and with the structure its range, but are floundering in the language symbols created by the event itself. Traditionally we speak of it as the

2. For representative statements from Reinhold, Fichte, Schiller, Hegel, and Schelling, see M. H. Abrams, *Natural Supernaturalism* (New York, 1971), 348–56. For the Hegel statement to Niethammer, see Johannes Hoffmeister, ed., *Briefe von und an Hegel*, 6th ed. (Hamburg, 1952), 1:253. For the Heine citation, see *Heines Werke in Fuenfzehn Teilen*, ed. Hermann Friedmann and Raimond Pissin (Berlin, n.d.), part 9, p. 276.

Ichphilosophie, or the *Identitaetsphilosophie,* or as the dialectical Logic of Being developed by Hegel as his capitalized "Method"; and we are justified in using these terms as long as we remain aware that they belong to the self-interpretation of the great German thinkers. Their usage will appear less justified, however, if we remember that the analytical validity of the terms is the point at issue, and that the terms appear in the internal polemics of the event and partially invalidate one another. We are on no safer ground if we use the comprehensive self-characterization as "transcendental idealism" because the conventional use of "idealism" would exclude the "materialism" of Karl Marx from the event. If, however, the Marxian system is to be included—perhaps as the first rolling of Heine's metaphorical thunder—the language of isms, and with it the great conflict of "idealism" and "materialism," becomes irrelevant. The analytical relevance would shift to the games played with the symbol "Being." We would have to understand the Marxian tactics of identifying the "Being" that determines history with the *Produktionsverhaeltnisse,* thereby putting Hegel's idealistically speculative "Being" on its feet, as an intellectual game made possible by Hegel's questionable use of the symbol "Being" as the Beginning of his System. If then we admit the structure of the event to be analytically a certain type of game played with the symbol "Being," of which the Marxian case is an instance, we may note with a new interest that in the twentieth century a German thinker of the rank of Martin Heidegger could, at least for a time, indulge in the phantasy of letting "Being" be forced into a new Parousia in reality by the national outbreak of a populist-racial movement. And if we have to understand the Marxian *Produktionsverhaeltnisse* and Heidegger's temporary National Socialism as equivalent deforming games, played according to the rules of Hegel's speculation on "Being," the event assumes proportions hitherto unsuspected.

The proportions will remain unclear as long as we are not clear about the criteria to be employed in judging the range of the event. But why do we suffer from this lack of clarity today, two hundred years after its outbreak? The question imposes itself pressingly, because the early contemporaries did not accept the spiritual revolt on its own terms at all but were moved to sarcastic comments. Heine was not alone in recognizing its revolutionary meaning, a meaning that could hardly be overlooked as it was proclaimed loudly by the authors of the "Systems" themselves; nor was he alone in poking fun at its grotesque implications. Jean Paul, for instance, was aroused quite early by the comic discrepancy between Fichte's speculative *Ich* and a man's consciousness of his self in bodily existence, and satirized it superbly in his *Clavis Fichtiana* of 1804, although expressing a perhaps ironical admiration for the aesthetic quality of Fichte's work. Four decades later, Kierkegaard engaged in his summary attack on the Fichtean and Hegelian speculative existence in the name of a Christian existentialism, developing in his "philosophical crumbs or a crumbly philosophy" the analytical importance of such symbols as anxiety, the instant (or moment), and existence that have become dominant symbols with the existentialist thinkers of the twentieth century. And a penetrating analysis, supported by the formidable historical apparatus of a competent theologian, was conducted by Ferdinand Christian Baur in his *Die Christliche Gnosis* of 1835, in which he placed Hegel's *Religionsphilosophie* in the context of the gnostic movements since antiquity. A broad basis thus had been laid on which further critical analysis could have been built. Why then has the event remained opaque nevertheless?

The reasons are to be found in the previously discussed ambiguities of resistance. The resisters to noetic truth are not necessarily its enemies; on the contrary, they may resist deformed symbolisms prevalent in their social environment and try to recover the truth obscured by those symbolisms. They may, however, be so strongly affected themselves by the prevalent disorder that their attempt at recovery, although eminently successful in other respects, will be conducted in the same style of self-assertive deformation that has motivated their resistance. The imaginative assertion in the creation of new symbols may have to carry the mortgage of a new self-assertion, and the will to find new symbols may derail into the will to dominate the reality symbolized. The new symbolism will then become a dictatorial imposition in the same imperial mode that aroused the revolt against the older symbolisms.

This is the problem of the German case. A solidly detailed, historically knowledgeable, comprehensive attack on symbols that have lost their meaning—the attempt to recover "the experience of consciousness" from which the emerging symbols derive their meaning—succumbs to deformation through the desire to dominate in the mode of thing-reality over the experience recovered. The ambiguity of formation-deformation on a new level of experiential differentiation is the reason why the analytical exploration of the event has remained inconclusive to this day. To accept the critical achievement on its own terms exposes one to the danger of falling into the trap of its deformation; roundly to reject the deformed result runs the danger of losing the critical achievement. The way out of the predicament does not lead through voluminous expositions and commentaries on the Systems in their expanse; the analysis has to concentrate on the peculiar structure of a deformed formative purpose that serves as the principle of their construction; and the ambiguous principle need not be unearthed from its application in the Systems, but is to be found in the programmatic declarations of their authors. The constructors of the Identity-System, especially Hegel, were masters of their problem; they knew what they wanted and expressed it with a clarity impaired only by the deformative component of their enterprise. They wanted to create, as Hegel formulated it in his *Phaenomenology,* a *Wissenschaft der Erfahrung des Bewusstseins*—a *Science of the Experience of Consciousness.* In order to illuminate the structure of ambiguity, I shall draw on representative statements from the *Vorrede* and *Einleitung* to Hegel's programmatic work.[3]

§2. Hegel I*

Hegel wanted to establish a "science of the experience of consciousness." The programmatic declaration determines the questions that have to be asked in the course of the analysis: To what extent did the program succeed? What did Hegel understand by "experience"? Which experiences were included in his analysis? Which were excluded? And how did the deformative will to power determine the inclusions and exclusions?

1. System vs. *Existential Tension*

The principle on which the ambiguous constructions rest is formulated by Hegel in the opening pages of the *Vorrede* (12). The true shape (*wahre Gestalt*) of truth is to be found in the form of

---

3. Hegel's formula, a "Science of the Experience of Consciousness," comes at the end of his *Einleitung* to the *Phaenomenology,* 74, in the Hoffmeister edition. All references to the *Phaenomenology* in the following pages are to that edition.

*Eric Voegelin died before writing the Hegel II segment of this chapter.

a "scientific system." Hegel proposes to himself to bring "philosophy" closer to its "true shape" so that it can abandon its name of "love of knowledge" and become "real knowledge." Stripped of such equivocal terms as "knowledge" and "science," Hegel's proposal to overcome the deformation of philosophy, painfully obvious under Enlightenment criticism, means the abolition of philosophy. The love of wisdom, the erotic tension toward the divine Beyond, a love that never seems to reach its object, this indefinite process that never comes to an end will have to be brought to its End by wisdom possessed in the shape of absolute knowledge, by a conclusive *Wissenschaft* beyond the inconclusive love. We are at the heart of the ambiguity. The program of a philosophy that makes an End of philosophy is the most glaring symptom of the intellectual confusion dominant at the time. Critically we have to say: The program excludes the experience of existential consciousness, of existence in the tension of the metaxy, from the "experience of consciousness."

2. *The Ambiguity of Dialectics*

If the tension of existence is not an experiential constant in the structure of consciousness, what then is really experienced? The answer is given in the concluding pages of the *Einleitung* to the *Phaenomenology* (69–75). Consciousness is to be conceived in the subject-object mode; it is consciousness of something (*etwas*). In a first approach, the something experienced is reality itself (*an sich*). In a second approach, however, when in the process of knowledge the something turns out to be different from what it was believed to be, the *Ansich* of reality becomes an *Ansich* for the experiencing subject (*fuer es*); behind the *Ansich* for consciousness there appears a second reality that is *an sich* for itself. Consciousness now has two objects (*Gegenstaende*), the "first *Ansich*" and "the second, *das Fuer-es-sein dieses Ansich*" (73). In discovering the "second object," then, consciousness discovers its own subjectivity to have changed from the first subject, which experienced the object as the first *Ansich*, into a second subject experiencing itself as in movement. "This dialectical movement which consciousness performs on itself, regarding both its knowledge and its object, inasmuch as there arises from it its new, true object, is properly [*eigentlich*] that which is called *experience*" (73). This movement, Hegel warns, must not be confused with the movement of knowledge advancing on the level of eonventionally so-called experience, in which the truth based on the observation of one thing can be externally falsified by the conflicting observation of another thing. The new object does not arise as a new external object, but through a "turning around of consciousness" (*Umkehrung des Bewusstseins*) (74). The *Umkehrung* is "our addition" (*unsere Zutat*); through the "addition," the "succession of the experiences of consciousness elevates itself to a course of science"; the succession is no such course of science for the consciousness on the "first" level of experience in the subject-object mode "that we contemplate" (74).

3. *The Deformation of the* Periagoge

The ambiguity of formation-deformation in Hegel's "experience," as well as the means for its expression, is apparent in the preceding passages. The structures he wants to clarify by his reflections on the *Ansich* and *Fuer-es* are recognizable. They are the paradox of intentionality-luminosity and the symbolic complex of consciousness-reality-language. The difficulties he encounters become tangible in the use of the symbol "*Umkehrung*" that recalls the *periagoge* of Plato's prisoner in the Cave, his turning around from the shadows on the wall and his ascent to the light. Hegel is in the position of the prisoner, openly in revolt against the shadows in the Cave of his age, be they doctrinal deformations of theology, propositional deformations of metaphysics or ontology, clever intellectualism, second-rate criticism or skepticism, ecstatically phantasizing exuberance, edifying sermonizing, or sentimental, thoughtless elevation. So far Hegel's movement is the same as the Platonic. If, however, we then look for the light shining from the Beyond that forces (*anangkoito*), directly or through a mediator, the prisoner to turn, we receive instead the information that the *periagoge* is *unsere Zutat*, our addition or addendum. The *periagoge* is not an assertive response but a self-assertive action.

At this point, the interpretation has to become linguistically pedantic, because the ambiguity of formation-deformation manifests itself in the ambiguity of Hegel's language.

4. *The Inversion of Formation-Deformation*

If the *Umkehrung* is a *Zutat*, an addition, it must be added to something that exists without the addendum. What then is this independently existent thing? In Hegel's context, it is the "experience" in the mode of the first *Ansich*, the "experience" that allows for treating the luminous symbolization of the It-reality in the mode of intentionality as a science of things given to a subject. It is the *natuerliche Erkenntnis* in its deformative application to the It-reality. By accepting the deformation of consciousness-reality as the "first" experience, the pathological case becomes the model by which the structures of consciousness are to be measured; the deformed Second Realities become the "first" reality to which formation will accrue as an addendum; the relational order of formation-deformation has been inverted. This peculiar inversion should be noted as a distinctive mark of the historical situation. It is symptomatic for the degree to which the experience and symbolization of existential consciousness had become unconscious in the public consciousness of intellectual debate at the time. The state of philosophy around 1800 was miserable, legitimizing the revolt of the best minds, even if the revolt culminated in its own deformation.

5. Pronominal Language

No less questionable is the pronominal language used to identify the actor in the process of acting. The turning around is *"unsere"* addition. Proceeding from the possessive to the personal pronoun: Who is the "we" who adds? In the Parable of the Cave, it is man in his personal and social existence who turns around, responding in his quest of truth to the drawing from the divine Beyond. Who then is Hegel's "we"? Is it man in his quest for truth, finding the truth by himself without the divine drawing? or is it the God who draws? Is it everyman who turns around, or is it only Hegel? And if only Hegel, does he turn around all by himself, or is he drawn by some other force? All of these questions manifestly exert their pressure on Hegel's programmatic declarations, but none of them is answered straightforwardly. The pronominal language is skillfully employed to hide what is really going on. Hegel does not pretend to be the only philosopher who has ever experienced the *Umkehrung*; on the contrary, he acknowledges the *Umkehrung* to be present wherever a skeptical voice is raised against a philosophical or theological symbolism that claims ultimacy for its symbols as the knowledge of truth in its *Ansich*. The truth is in motion; even more, as we have seen, the motion is the truth. Every symbolism that claims ultimate knowledge of the *Ansich* as an object "sinks off" (*sinkt herab*) for consciousness to a *Fuer-das Bewusstsein-Sein des Ansich* (74). "This circumstance" (*dieser Umstand*) is the "necessity" (*Notwendigkeit*) that guides the shapes of consciousness in their sequence. "Only this necessity itself, or the *genesis* of the new object, offering itself to a consciousness that does not know what happens to it, is what occurs [*fuer uns*] as-it-were behind its back." Through this necessity there enters into the movement of consciousness "a factor [*Moment*] of the *Ansich-oder Fuerunssein* that is not present to the consciousness engaged in the experience itself." While the genesis (*die Enstehung*) of the new object occurs behind the back of consciousness, however, the resulting product (*das Enstandene*) is a content *fuer es*, for consciousness; but what we conceive (*begreifen*) of this content is only the formality (*das Formelle*) of its pure genesis. *Fuer es*, for consciousness, the product exists only in the mode of object; *fuer uns*, it is at the same time movement and becoming (74).

6. Hegel's Pronomina and Plato's Nomina

In the passages just reported, Hegel enacts the ambiguous role of a prisoner in the Cave who takes over the control of the *periagoge*. If we want to understand the meaning of this game with the pronomina, we must relate them to the nomina, i.e., to the recognizably Platonic symbols the pronominal language is meant to eclipse. We have previously noted the general purpose of bringing the inconclusive process of philosophy in the Platonic sense to its capitalized End by the creation of a speculative System of Science. We then had to note the transmogrification of Plato's *periagoge* into the *Umkehrung*, with the odd consequence of inverting the relation of formation and deformation: the formative force becoming an addendum, while the propositional deformation of philosophical symbols, the "shadows," become the primary, *natuerliche*, "experience." And now we have to note the divine light that radiates from the Beyond and forces the prisoner to turn around transmogrified into a *Notwendigkeit*, a necessity that operates behind the back of the prisoners' consciousness and forces "us" to produce one propositionally deformed, intentionalist shadow in the Cave after another, until Hegel appears and makes an end of the unconscious productions by raising into consciousness their meaning as a millennial process of the absolute spirit with the purpose of revealing itself absolutely at last in the System of Science.

7. The Inversion of Consciousness into Unconsciousness

The deformation of Platonic symbols reveals the extraordinary conflict with reality in Hegel's programmatic declarations. Hegel wants to create a "science of the experience of consciousness" and proceeds by eliminating from consciousness the philosopher's experience of being drawn into his quest for truth by the divine reality from the Beyond. The drawing becomes an indeterminate "necessity" behind the back of consciousness; what enters consciousness is only the body of literary symbols produced by the "necessity." What is implied in this construction is so unbelievably grotesque that one hardly dares to put it into plain language: Plato's work of a lifetime in exploring the experience of the quest, of its human-divine movements and countermovements, of the ascent to the height of the Beyond and the descent into the cosmic depth of the soul, the anamnetic meditations, the analysis of existence in the tensions between life and death, between Nous and passions, between truth and opinionated dreams, the Vision (in the *Laws*) of the divine formative force—this overwhelmingly conscious drama of the quest, this reality of consciousness and its luminous symbolization in a philosopher's existence, is excluded from the "experience of consciousness" and relegated to an unconscious "necessity" behind Plato's back. Together with the consciousness of noetic existence and its symbolization, there is thrown out of consciousness Plato's reflective distance to his work, his consciousness of his work as an event that marks a Before and After in the history of truth without putting an end to the quest for truth. What remains for "consciousness" is a body of literary work, to be understood in a fundamentalist manner as a set of propositions in the subject-object mode, with Hegel conveniently forgetting Plato's energetic declarations that anybody who understood him in this manner had not understood what he was doing.

8. The Public Unconscious (Jung-Kerényi)

But we are not engaged in a critique of Hegel. We seek to unravel the ambiguities of a program, representative of the intellectual confusion of its age and determining further confusions up to our own time. At present, we are concerned with confusions caused by changes in the meaning of "consciousness" and "unconscious." If the intentionalist deformation of consciousness through the act of reflection is accepted as the model of consciousness, the formative experiences of the structure of consciousness will not fit the model; they must be excluded from consciousness. Since the exclusion, however, does not abolish their reality, and since the program is formatively meant to recover the experiences lost at the time, we are confronted with the odd result that the "experience of consciousness" is indeed recovered but, when recovered, has to be classified as a type of "unconsciousness."

The phenomena of this class are well known. For a striking instance I refer to the famous studies of Jung and Karl Kerényi on the Divine Child, the Kore, and the Eleusinian mystery, published in 1942 under the title *Einfuehrung in das Wesen der Mythologie.* The excellent studies of Kerényi on the range of the previously too-little-known symbolism of the Divine Child reveal its meaning as the experience of new formative life emerging from a dangerously resistant It-reality, to be cruelly destroyed, only to rise in a new beginning, i.e, the experience of the immortal It-reality comprehending the mortal reality of things, or, in Jung's explicit formulation, the experience of "beginning and end." The Divine Child is a conscious symbolization of the paradox of reality, of the story reality has to tell of itself through the story told by man. The analytical studies of Jung, then, confirm the "reality" of the symbolism through its reappearance, in the form of fragmentalized parts, in the dreams and visions of patients who suffer from mental disturbances because they have lost these experiences from their consciousness.

But the more one agrees with the important empirical findings of the two scholars, the more one is astonished to see them classify the symbols explored as "unconscious." Does the classification mean that the ancient symbolizers were not aware of the experiences they were expressing when they were creating their symbols? Did the participants in the Eleusinian rituals not know why they flocked to their performance? why they wanted to be initiated? and were the initiates unconscious of the mystery revealed to them, of the mystery of immortality comprehending mortality? Were they just sitting or standing there, drawing "archetypes" from the "collective unconscious"? In short: Had the members of the mystery cult really to wait for Jung and Kerényi to discover what they were unconsciously conscious of?

These pointed questions do not purpose to denigrate Jung's symbols of consciousness and unconscious as nonsense, but to bring their ambiguity into focus. The absurdity of characterizing the ancient symbolizers as "unconsciously conscious" reveals its sense as soon as we re-invert the inversion and characterize the modern symbolizers as "consciously unconscious." The modern symbolizer is really "unconscious" but is becoming aware of it and is trying to recover "consciousness" through the study of the myth that offers richer insights into the movements and structures of consciousness than the intellectual babble of his time. This re-inversion of the inversion, I should like to stress, is not my "addendum" to Jung's categorization but renders as exactly as possible his own consciousness of being unconscious. "Psychology," he insists, "transfers the archaic speech of myth into a modern mythologem— not yet, of course, recognized as such—which constitutes one element of the myth 'science'" (146). In Jung's "psychology" we witness the ambiguous "consciousness" becoming aware of being "unconscious," as well as the valiant endeavor to recover consciousness through the study of its manifestations in history, and the regrettably not-quite-successful struggle for the language that will express the newly differentiated experience. Of the ambiguous "modern mythologems" developed by Jung I shall retain the symbol "unconscious" in one of its component meanings, using it, as I have done already, to denote a socially dominant state of consciousness deformed by oblivion that causes personal and public disturbances of order. In this sense it will be used to denote not only the contemporary state of the public unconscious but also the comparable states in other cultural situations, as for instance the Hellenic state of the public unconscious against which Plato revolted.[4]

9. The Act of Imaginative Oblivion

In Jung's case, we are at the stage where a representative carrier of the ambiguous consciousness is becoming conscious of being

---

4. C. G. Jung and Karl Kerényi, *Einfuehrung in das Wesen der Mythologie*, 4th ed. (Zurich, 1951). The translation is R. F. C. Hull, ed., *Essays on a Science of Mythology* (Princeton, 1969), 98.

unconscious; in the case of Hegel's program, we are at the stage where a representative thinker, resisting the deformations dominant at the time, reconstructs the public unconscious of the age, on a differentiated level, as a new type of consciousness. The program, although it is clear about its intent, remains ambiguously opaque because it fails to digest analytically the various strands of experience converging in it. One of these strands expressed itself in the grotesque of inverting Plato's noetic consciousness into a state of unconsciousness; I had to stress it, because Hegel had made it central in his program. But why did he engage in the grotesque act of throwing out Plato's symbolization of noetic consciousness through the myth as "scientifically worthless" (57), while retaining the very structure of the myth in his transformations of the *periagoge* into the *Umkehrung,* as well as of the existentially formative movement in the metaxy toward the divine Beyond into a "necessity" operating "behind the back" of the thinker? Such transformations cannot be explained as simple misunderstandings caused by careless reading of the sources: They rather presuppose the noetic structure, together with its Platonic symbolization, to be very much present in Hegel's consciousness, while at the same time this presence is willed not to be present. We are faced with a deliberate act of imaginative oblivion and have to ask for the experiential reasons why the symbolization of existence in tension toward the Beyond was obnoxious to Hegel as the thinker who representatively articulated the unconscious of his age. What is the necessity behind his back that forces him to deform the Nous?

10. The Self-Analysis of Activist Consciousness

In answering these questions we do not have to engage in extended psychoanalysis. Hegel's self-analysis of his unconscious is concentrated with admirable clarity in his opposition of the symbol *"Geist"* to the Platonic Nous. First of all, he declares programmatically: "That truth is real only as a System, or that the substance is essentially subject, is expressed in the perception [*Vorstellung*] which pronounces the Absolute as *Geist*—this sublimest concept which belongs to the modern age [*neuere Zeit*] and its religion" (24). When we ask for the historical context and meaning of this modern symbol, we receive the information (in the chapter on Boehme, in *Geschichte der Philosophie,* 2:300): It is "the Protestant principle to place the world of the Intellect [*Intellektuel Welt*] into one's own mind [*Gemueth*], and to see, know, and feel in one's own self-consciousness all that was previously Beyond." When the Protestant principle has ultimately reconciled the former diremption into this world and the Beyond; when the historical antecedents of self-consciousness, the Nous of Anaxagoras, the Ideas of Plato, and the last remnant of the Beyond, the Kantian *Ding-an-sich*, have been conceptually penetrated and absorbed into the immanence of the self-moving consciousness; when in this process the concept has become Being, and the being Concept, then the realm of the *Geist* has come into its truth (46). The realm in its truth, finally, is presented by Hegel in his *Logik*. Of this presentation and its content he says: "This realm is the truth, as it is without veil in and for itself. One can express oneself therefore in this manner: its content is the presentation of God as he is in his eternal Being [*ewiges Wesen*] before the creation of nature and a finite *Geist*" (1:31). The passage transmogrifies the Gospel of Saint John 1:1. According to the Gospel, the Logos was in the Beginning with God; now the Beginning turns out to be no more than a beginning in time that comes to its full revelation, to its true modern End, in the *Geist* of Hegel's *Logik*.[5]

There is more to Hegel's unconscious, however, than the proclamation of the *Geist* as a modern, Protestant principle suggests, for he lets the "modern" principle cover by its topical head a variety of hermetic, apocalyptic, gnostic, and Neoplatonic strands of experience. Even Plato, although his myth is worthless, has to be praised for his *Parmenides*, "the greatest work of art of ancient dialectics," rightly held at times to be "the true revelation and positive expression of the divine life" (57). The laudatory phrase comes close to Hegel's self-praise of his *Logik*. Closest to his programmatic *Geist*, however, comes Marsilio Ficino's programmatic statement, in the introduction to his translation of the *Corpus Hermeticum*, that the Divine Mind "may glow into our mind and we may contemplate the order of all things as they exist in God," a statement that was probably unknown to Hegel. We are reminded of the gnostic desire, condemned by Irenaeus, to read in God as in a book.

---

5. Hegel, *Vorlesungen ueber die Geschichte der Philosophie* (volume 19 of the Jubilee edition edited by Herman Glockner), 3:300. See also Hegel, *Wissenschaft der Logik,* ed. Georg Lasson (Hamburg, 1963), part 1, p. 31.

Nevertheless, whatever strands of experience we may add, the dominant in the symbol *"Geist"* remains a paracletic eschatology, the vision of a descent of the Spirit that will achieve what the Petrine and Pauline Christianities have not achieved—i.e., the ultimately salvational Parousia of the Beyond in this world. To indulge in this phantasy, and to propose in the course of its activist realization the abolition of philosophy, required a considerable amount of unconsciousness regarding the treatment of this problem by the Hellenic, Hellenistic, and medieval thinkers. We now have to identify the trauma that caused this peculiar state of activist unconsciousncss in Hegel's time.

11. The Trauma of the Orthodox Environment

Hegel, like so many of his contemporaries and successors up to Nietzsche, Jung, and Heidegger, had been the victim of his upbringing under the pressures of an orthodox environment. He had been exposed, with an intense experience of resistance, to the deformation of the complex of consciousncss-reality-language, to the deformation of It-reality into thing-reality, of luminosity into intentionality, of symbols into definitional concepts. The Beyond, the symbol created by Plato to express his experience of divine reality as formatively present in the participatory movements in the metaxy, had become a spatially located object, a *Jenseits* of this world; and the Platonic symbolization of the divine Nous as Being beyond finite beings had been transformed into the concept of a being thing beyond the being things. In Hegel's language, the experiential symbols Beyond and Being have become entities with a definite article, *das Jenseits, das Sein.* Finally, the linguistic deformation made it possible for the symbol Being to appear as the predicate in propositions in which the God of Christian orthodoxy had become the subject, as in *Gott ist das Sein.* Noetic and pneumatic, Hellenic and Judaeo-Christian symbols had been transformed into intentionalist concepts to be manipulated by propositional thinkers. It is Hegel's irreversible achievement to have thoroughly understood the dominant deformation of symbols; it is Hegel's grandiose failure to have attempted a solution by fusing the It-reality and the thing-reality into the new symbolism of the *Sein*, a subject that unfolds its substance in the historical process "dialectically" until it reaches its *eschaton*, its End, in fully articulate conceptualization of its self-consciousness, thus out-comprehending the comprehending reality.

12. God: The Senseless Sound

Although it is difficult, if not impossible, to present either the achievement or the failure in Hegel's own words, considering the ambiguity of his language, it is possible to identify the point at which the dominant deformation arouses his acute resistance: The traumatic point is manifest in his preoccupation with the proposition *Gott ist das Sein.*

In this proposition, "God" is for Hegel the subject in two meanings. First, he is the grammatical subject of which Being is predicated; and second, he is a subject in the sense of a self-reflective consciousness. As a grammatical subject, God is for Hegel a superfluous entity. If sentences begin with "God"—as in "God is the Eternal," or "the Love," or "the Being," or "the One"—then God is a senseless sound, a mere name of which only the predicate says what he is; "this empty beginning [of the sentence] becomes real knowledge only in its end." One might rightly ask, therefore, why one should not speak of the predicative meaning alone, "without adding the *senseless* sound" (22). Hence, in a philosophical discussion it might be helpful "to avoid the name of God" (54). As a grammatical subject, thus, God has to surrender his place to Being. Nevertheless, even in the grammatical place God still has some use. The incriminated propositions reflect "the need to imagine the Absolute as a Subject." It is true, the propositions only posit the Subject but do not present it in its self-reflective movement; but the word "God" at least indicates that not "a being or essence or something general at large is posited but a something that is self-reflected, a Subject." But even this concession might be too generous, for the image "God" no more than "anticipates the Absolute as Subject, as it posits it only as a quiescent point," not in the reality of its Being as a conceptual "movement" (23). To supply Hegel's Being, which otherwise would be no more than a "generality," with the movement of the divine Intellect appears to be the last, and not too certain, service God can render.

80

13. Ambiguity and Paradoxic Validity

The famous, provocative passages will remain analytically unintelligible, unless the experiences that have been deformed by the ambiguous act of resistance are identified.

What imposes itself on our attention, first of all, is the questionable game with the symbol "subject." If its ambiguity were dismissed as a simple equivocation, invalidating the construction, the underlying experiential issue would be missed. We must distinguish between the experientially valid component of the equivocation and its deformation. What I just called the experientially valid component we encountered in our own analysis of consciousness. On the one hand, the subject of consciousness intended reality as its object, motivating the symbol of a thing-reality; on the other hand, the acts of bodily located consciousness turned out to be events in the It-reality and, under this experiential aspect, had to be propositionally "predicated" of the It-reality as their "subject." The equivocation was not a logical mistake but the linguistic manifestation of the paradox of consciousness, of intentionality and luminosity, that extends its structure into the problems of reality, language, and imagination. The story of the quest for truth speaks a language, the language of the tale, in which the symbols expressing the experiences become subjects in sentences with predicates as if they were "things" with properties. If the consciousness of the experiences that have engendered the symbols is not preserved or restored, the narrative-event tension in the story can induce literalist misunderstandings. Hegel, we must acknowledge, has encountered and apprehended the problem; in fact, he has engaged in some very important observations concerning the language of the tale, as we shall see in due course. If his insights have remained ambiguous nevertheless, the reason must be sought in his resistance to the deformed symbol "God" without a sufficient analysis of the experiential reasons for its formation or of the historical modes of its deformation.

14. God: The Experience of His Death

Hegel is a historically knowledgeable and analytically formidable thinker. When he declares the symbol "God" to be a senseless sound, religious indignation would be as fatuous a response as would the display of enlightened pleasure. When a Hegel is ambiguous, his ambiguity reflects a fundamental problem in the structure of consciousness that has become opaque in his time. While the radical manifestation of the opacity in Hegel's statements is a specifically "modern" event, the paradoxic structure of revelatory symbols in the background, as well as the potential of their deformation, has burdened the language of the gods with its problems as far back as our written records go, i.e., to the Egyptian third millennium B.C. Moreover, problems of this class have attained a new level of acuteness ever since the symbol "God" has become differentiated in the so-called monotheistic sense. The opacity in Hegel's time must be understood in its historical context as the culmination of a millennial struggle with the paradoxes of divine revelation. The only critically permissible response in this situation is the analysis of the sense the symbol "God" made when it emerged from the experience of reality in Hellenic antiquity, an analysis that will have to include the problems of formation and deformation surrounding its genesis. This analysis will be given in the immediately following sections of the present chapter.

Before engaging in this analysis, however, we must identify the characteristic in Hegel's ambiguity that makes it representative for a "modern" historical phase in the millennial struggle. This characteristic has frequently been observed in an incidental manner, even on the level of jokes; but it has never been made analytically thematic, as far as I know, in a manner that would do justice to Hegel's range of historical consciousness. I shall call this representative characteristic the serio-comic trait of the modern God-is-dead movement.

The movement must be taken seriously: The terse formula on the "senseless sound" is not idiosyncratic but must be accepted as the authoritative expression of the God-is-dead movement that characterizes a period of Western modernity, now lasting for about three hundred years. The historical phenomena are well known. I mention only, before Hegel, the Enlightenment atheism, its activist radicalization in the Marquis de Sade's *Encore un effort, Français . . .* (1793), and the parallel, depressive-resistant counter-dream of Jean Paul's *Rede des toten Christus vom Weltgebaeude herab, dass kein Gott sei* (1794); and since Hegel, the variety of positivist, antitheistic methodologies, the projection psychology of Feuerbach and Marx, Nietzsche's reflection on "the murder of

God," and the existentialist wave of God-is-dead literature in the twentieth century.

But the movement has also its comic touch: The God who is declared dead is alive enough to have kept his undertakers nervously busy by now for three centuries. Yet the life he is leading, before and after his death, is troubled and complicated. When interrogated by eminent thinkers, he does not seem to be sure whether he is a substance or a subject (Spinoza/Hegel), or perhaps both, or whether he perhaps does not exist at all, whether he is personal or impersonal, whether conscious or unconscious, whether rational or irrational, whether spirit only or matter too (Spinoza), whether he is perhaps only a regulative idea (Kant), whether he is identical with himself or not, or whether he is the identity of identity and nonidentity (Hegel), whether he is an ontological or a theological being, or both, or whether he is something entirely different (Heidegger). What is absolute in this ambiguous debate about the Absolute is its deadly seriousness. The only one permitted to laugh in the situation appears to be God.

15. Mortality and Immortality of the Gods

Neither the seriousness of the God-is-dead movement, nor its touch of comedy, can be denied. Both characteristics derive from the paradox in the complex of consciousness-reality-language. The language of the gods symbolizes the experienced Parousia of the Beyond. Divine reality is experienced as present in the divine-human ordering movements of the soul and, at the same time, as something "beyond" its concrete presence. In the analysis of Saint Thomas, for instance, there appears the personal God who bears the proper name "God," but behind the God who speaks his Word and hears the word of prayer, there looms the nameless, the impersonal, the tetragrammatic God. The God who is experienced as concretely present remains the God beyond his presence. The language of the gods, thus, is fraught with the problem of symbolizing the experience of a not-experientiable divine reality. While the imaginative symbols expressing this experience are never intentionalist concepts defining the nature of a god, they have linguistically the appearance of language in the mode of thing-reality. As a consequence, if the language of the gods is misconstrued as a conceptual language referring to a divine entity "beyond" the experience of the

Beyond and its Parousia, the gods must die when their language is superseded in the differentiating process of the quest for truth by a more adequate language. The historical scene becomes littered with dead gods. If, however, this mistake is not made, if the consciousness of experience and symbolization remains alive, or is gained, the succession of the gods becomes a series of events to be remembered as the history of the Parousia of the living, divine Beyond. Not the Beyond but its Parousia in the bodily located consciousness of questioning man, the experience of the not-experientiable divine reality, has history: the history of truth emerging from the quest for truth. Under this aspect, the serious effort of the quest for truth acquires the character of a divine comedy.

16. The Language of the Gods: Death-Parousia-Remembrance

Hegel was well aware of the paradoxic and reflectively distancing structures in the language of the gods. I shall enumerate the principal issues on which he expressed his consciousness in the *Phaenomenology:*

(a) He knew that the gods were not dying for the first time in history when they died in his "modern age." In the ancient civilizations the gods had died, too. In a variation on the Stoic *theologia tripertita,* in the three chapters on "Natural Religion," "Art Religion," and "Revealed Religion," he remembered the gods who had lived and died in the past. In particular he reflected on the death of the Olympian gods through dissolution in the "clouds" of Aristophanes' comedy (517–20; see also the remarks on the *komische Bewusstsein,* 523).

(b) Hegel knew, furthermore, that the gods, even though they die in history as the victims of the differentiating process of truth, have to be "remembered" as living gods because their plurality in co-existence and succession is the Parousia of the living Beyond (508). In his own case, although he formally declared God himself to have died (*dass Gott gestorben ist*) "in the abstraction of the divine *Wesen*" in which his doctrinaire contemporaries indulged (523, 546), Hegel knew that the dead God was alive enough to celebrate a Parousia in the System of Science: In the *Phaenomenology,* the *theologia tripertita* is followed by this Parousia in the concluding chapter on "The Absolute Knowledge"—a Parousia even if it is libidinously deformed by Hegel's self-assertive speculation.

(c) Most important finally, as a connoisseur of the historical antecedents to his own analytic efforts, Hegel was familiar with the Hesiodian symbolism of Remembrance (507–8). The divine-human Mnemosyne, the symbol that we owe to the creative imagination of Hesiod, inchoatively differentiated the reflective distance of consciousness to the paradoxic process of reality. Hesiod symbolized, within the limits of his compact language, the "remembering" distance to the experience of reality as a Whole, and in particular to the experience of the not-experientiable divine Beyond and its Parousia in the gods who live and die. By differentiating the experience of reflective distance he opened consciousness for the process of reality as an unfinished story. Hegel, in his turn, understood Remembrance quite well as the constituent of historical consciousness; but he wanted to finish the story. For this purpose the noetic insight into the paradoxic structure of reality had to be self-assertively deformed into the mastery of the paradox as a "thing"; and with the mystery transformed into a "thing" to be mastered, the distancing Remembrance that had opened the historical horizon could become the instrument of its closure through the pretense that everything worth remembering about the process of truth in reality had been remembered. With these assumptions taken for granted, the paradoxic process of the quest for truth could be assumed to be finished, and the unfinished story could be brought to its End in the System of Science.

Hegel's deformation of certain structures of consciousness, however, must not obscure the fact that he acted in revolt against the even worse deformation of the same structures in the public unconscious that surrounded him socially. He could deform fundamental experiences only by first rediscovering them in opposition to symbols that had lost the experiential source of their meaning and, as a consequence, had become a dead body of ideas and opinions. Hence, the preceding enumeration should not be read as a critique of Hegel but, on the contrary, as an attempt to clarify and stress his achievement. His rediscovery of the experiential source of symbolization, as well as his identification of the fundamental problems in the structure of consciousness, is irreversible. What must be reversed is his deformation of the problems identified. The two following sections—"Hesiod's Mnemosyne" and "Remembrance of Reality"—will analyze, in their original undeformed form, phases in the process of truth that Hegel, as the above enumeration has shown, acknowledged as antecedents to his own understanding of consciousness. By this method it will be possible, I hope, to restore some sense to sounds that have become senseless.

§3. Hesiod's Mnemosyne

Hesiod develops the symbolism of Mnemosyne in his *Theogony*, in the Invocations of the Muses. The *Theogony* is remarkable for its beginning, not with one, but with three Invocations. I assume them to form a unit of meaning. As a unit they are devised to deal with the various aspects of "beginning" an account, i.e., a Remembrance, of reality and its structures that is supposed to be true. In order to warrant its truth, the account has to "begin" with an inquiry into the structure of the remembering quest for truth itself. The noetic responsibility of the quest, thus, becomes thematic. Under this thematic aspect, the threefold "beginning" of the *Theogony* may be compared to Hegel's "Invocations" of the *Geist* in the *Vorrede* and *Einleitung* to the *Phaenomenology*. I shall trace the unfolding of the symbolism through the three Invocations in their sequence.[6]

1. The Parousia of the Muses—Mediation of Divine Truth

In the first Invocation (vv. 1–35), the Heliconian Muses are praised as the divine mediators of the truth about reality, i.e., "about the things that shall come and the things that were before" (32). The poet experiences the truth of reality as a divine Beyond, not to be grasped by intentional consciousness in its *Ansich*, but to be mediated through the Parousia of the Muses. This divine-human movement in the metaxy is reported as the existential, revelatory event in which the truth of reality originates (26–28). The event, then, is accompanied by the assurance that the present revelation will be truer than what sometimes was revealed to and by the poet's predecessors. Previous symbols can become false (*pseudea*) when, in the process of differentiation, they are superseded by more

---

6. References to Hesiod in the following pages cite the Loeb Classical Library edition of *Theogony*, ed. and trans. Hugh G. Evelyn-White.

adequate imagery (*alethea*); Hesiod is conscious of the true-false tension in imaginative symbolization (27–28). And finally, the truth the Muses order him to sing is "of the race of the blessed eternal beings [*eonta*] but of themselves first and last" (33–34); there is no song of the gods without their mediated presence in the Muses. Although the existential event has revealed itself in its happening, nothing is revealed as yet beyond the fact of its happening. We are at the stage of analysis that, on another occasion, I have pressed into the succinct formula: The fact of revelation is its content [*NSP*, 78].

2. *The Muses Remember Their Divinity to the Gods*

In the second Invocation (36–104), Hesiod distances the event by reflecting on the experiential structure in Music revelation. The first Invocation has ordered him to praise the Muses first and last; he now obeys: "Let us begin with the Muses" (36).

The Muses are the daughters of Mnemosyne, of Remembrance, from her union with Zeus in his extended act of "forgetting the troubles and reposing from cares" (53–55). Their genesis as well as their function are imagined as internal to the divine reality itself. The scene of their begetting is the Olympian Beyond, or rather a Jovian Beyond superior to the Olympian, for their begetting is stressed to have taken place "far from the immortals" (57); and when they are born, they have to sing their remembering song to the Olympians, but above all to Zeus, "the father of gods and men" (36–43). The Muses, thus, mediate divinity primarily to the gods themselves, and only secondarily to men by inspiring the ordering word of princes and singers (79–104). But what is this odd Remembrance, internal to the divine Beyond? of what have the Muses to remember the gods—if we may use the verb in a sense that has become archaic?

The Olympians have to be remembered of their existence as the presence of divine order, victorious over the disorder of the older gods from whom they stem and who still are alive. Remembrance, in the sense of the Hesiodian symbol, does not recollect a dead past but "remembers" a presence that is a living presence only if it is fully conscious of its ordering victory over forces that once were just as victoriously present. In his compact language of the myth, Hesiod expresses his insight into Remembrance as the reflective distance to the existentially ordering event in the metaxy. The reflectively distancing Mnemosyne is the dimension of consciousness in which the presence of the Beyond, experienced as the ordering force in the event, gains the reality of its Parousia in the language of the gods. The "existence" of the gods is the presence of the divine Beyond in the language symbols that express its moving Parousia in the experience of the not-experientiable ordering force in the existential event. With Hesiod, we are touching the limits of symbolization in the language of the gods: There are no gods without a Beyond of the gods.

We are at the stage of differentiating analysis at which the relation between the gods and their Beyond is becoming noetically problematic. In the first Invocation, the Heliconian Muses mediate the truth of the Olympian Beyond by inspiring the Hesiodian song. In the second Invocation, the Olympian Beyond acquires an internal structure. The immortals appear to be in doubt about their own Parousia as the victoriously ordering gods and have to be remembered of their divine presence by the Muses. But there are no Muses as long as they are not begotten by Zeus on Mnemosyne. A Jovian Beyond differentiates from the gods of the Olympian Beyond. But even Zeus is not the ultimate Beyond. Although he is immortal, he has to be born to be immortal; and when he has gained his victory over the older born gods, he has to be "remembered" of his victorious presence. Moreover, even after his victory, one should note, his existence remains so intensely burdened with the struggle for order against resistant forces that he has to seek repose from his cares in the union with Mnemosyne. The Muses let the god "forget" for a while the continuing struggle by putting the accent of their remembering song, reassuringly, on the ultimately victorious presence of ordering, divine reality. Within the divine struggle for truly ordered existence, the Muses intone a visionary song of divinely true existence beyond the struggle. Their song has an apocalyptic theme; and the apocalypse is sung, not to men only, but to Zeus himself. The Jovian existence, with the precarious consciousness of its presence, is a Parousia, i.e., a revelatory event within a comprehending divine reality. Zeus himself has a Beyond. The noetic pressure in Hesiod's quest lets him pile Beyond on Beyond in the medium of the myth, a process foreshadowing its culmination in Plato's vision of the noetic *epekeina* beyond all being things, including the gods and Zeus himself. Even when the vision of the divine One is achieved, however, neither Plato, nor after him Plotinus, would deny the divinity of the older gods. The older gods become "old" under noetic pressure, but they remain immortal. They will not die. Why not?

3. *The Tale of the Divine Things* (ta eonta)

The answer to this question is the theme of the third invocation (105–15). Hesiod experiences the Beyond, in the sense of the generating and formative force in all reality, so compactly present in the generated and formed structures, ranging from the primordial triad of Chaos, Earth, and Eros to the Olympian gods, that the Parousia of the force is not sufficiently differentiated from its Beyond. The structures are still compactly divine. While the noetic pressure in his thought is manifest, it does not imaginatively advance to a symbolization of the noetic Beyond. This intermediate stage of mythospeculation has the advantage that Hesiod is not plagued with the temptation of erecting the Beyond into an intentionalist entity; hence, he does not have to resist, like Hegel, the hypostatized *Jenseits* of a hypostatized Parousia; his gods have just enough of a Beyond to be in need of being remembered of their divinity. In a language more differentiated than Hesiod's, but less deformed than Hegel's, one would have to say that the gods are immortal because they are born from the participatory presence of the Beyond in the divine-human tension of the metaxy, but that the immortals partake of temporality because they are also born from the participatory presence of the responsively imaginative, human consciousness in the limitation of its bodily located, temporal mortality. The questing struggle for the truth of reality is the struggle of reality for its truth; it occurs within reality and involves the whole of the hierarchy of being, from the basic material structures to the formative experience of the not-experientiable Beyond. Immortality is experienced by mortals; what has been born in time will die in time; its immortality is gained from its participation in the story of the It-reality.

With this last formulation we are returning to Hesiod's symbols. For there is no participation in the story of the It-reality to be told unless it is "remembered"; and how can it be "remembered" unless the participatory character of the story is really experienced in the present experience of existential reality? Remembrance in the Hesiodian sense constitutes consciousness as the consciousness of its own story in the struggle of the metaxy, of its genesis as part of a comprehending story. If the present of existential reality were not remembered as a metaleptic story, there would be no story of anything. If, however, the story of the struggle in the metaxy, told in reflective distance, constitutes the structure of consciousness in the "present," it thereby constitutes its past and future as "Presents" in their own time. The participatory story, if remembered in the present of existence, expands into the story of its past and future as the story of the relations between its "presents"—within the limits, of course, of the knowledge concretely available at the time. I suspect that the much-discussed problem of "historicity" has found, in Hesiod's Remembrance, an analytical symbol difficult to improve upon.

The Muses of the third Invocation are expected to remember the genesis of the gods, as they are born (*exegenonto*) from Earth, from starry Heaven, from gloomy Night, and briny Sea (105–7). The "gods" born from this source, although they are called to bring order to the world and themselves in justice (*Erga* 1–10; *Theogony* 71–73), have not created the world they are supposed to order. The tension of creation-salvation is present in Hesiod's experience of reality. In order to render their account of creatively divine presence in the process of reality, however, the Muses have to use Hesiod's language of compact divinity, i.e., a language of the gods that has not yet sufficiently differentiated the tensions of Beginning-Beyond and Parousia-Beyond. The symbols at Hesiod's, and the Muses', disposition are too compact a means of imaginative expression to be quite adequate to the degree of noetic differentiation the experience has achieved. As a consequence, the story told by the Muses has to struggle with certain problems of symbolization. The story is supposed to tell the epiphany of structures in reality as a manifestation of divine creativity: The structures experienced range, as in the book of Genesis, from the material forms of Earth and Heaven to the formative movement of the divine Beyond in the metaxy; moreover, as in Genesis, the Muses are requested to tell this story of creational reality "from the beginning" (*ex arches*) (115); and yet, they are supposed to tell the story of divine creativity without symbolizing the divine creative power beyond all being things. But how does a Beginning begin if there is no acting Beyond and nothing to be acted upon? Hesiod, it appears, has to cope with the same problem as Hegel, with the problem of telling a story that presupposes the experience of the Beyond without symbolizing it. Still, there is an important difference between the two cases. For Hesiod, experience and symbolization are imaginatively moving toward the differentiation of the Beyond, whereas Hegel tries to annul a differentiation achieved by committing it to imaginative oblivion. A few observations on the ambiguities in Hesiod's compact, but remembering, language will make the ambiguities in Hegel's differentiated, but oblivious, construction more intelligible.

The dominant symbols in Hesiod's story are the "gods" (*theoi*) and the "things" or "beings" (*eonta*). The symbol "gods" represents, above all, the Olympians, but also their existential Remembrance, i.e., Mnemosyne and the Muses; it further pertains to the "gods" from whom the Olympians descended, i.e., to Ouranos and Kronos, but also to such sidelines as the Cyclopes and the Titans; and finally, it has to embrace the originating triad of the divine succession, i.e., the triad of Chaos-Gaia-Eros. While the relations between the successive strata of the "gods" are symbolized as genetic in the biological sense, the beginning of the genealogical line remains ambiguous. Each member of the primordial triad, it is true, is accorded a specific rank through praising epithets: Chaos is distinguished as the firstborn of them all; Eros, then, as "the most beautiful among the deathless gods"; and especially Gaia, the Earth, as "the safe genetic seat [*hedos asphales*] of all things [*panton*]" (116–20). Still, none of them is the creative source of the other two; nor is there any creative actor behind them, or any material on which he could have acted. Chaos, as Werner Jaeger has stressed, is no such material; it is neither a Platonic *chora*, nor a Hebrew *tohu wabohu*, but the yawning chasm between Heaven and Earth. The members of the triad are inexorably self-genetic; their creative force is immanent to themselves. This ambiguity of a self-genetic reality, then, is compounded by the ambiguous relations between the symbols "gods" and "things." The Muses are supposed to tell the story of "the things [*eonta*] that are, that shall be, and that were before" (38). But what are these *eonta*? When the Muses tell of earth, of rivers and sea, of heaven and the stars, and of the gods born from them, it sounds as if the cosmic structures mentioned were the "things" from whom the "gods" are born (108–11), but when we trace the genetic line back to the self-genetic triad there can be no doubt that the cosmic structures are "gods," too. Moreover, when the Olympians themselves are called "the race of the immortal *eonta* that are forever" (33, 105), "gods" and "things" appear to become synonyms. But if they are synonyms, what then are men? Do they become "gods" when the Muses have to sing of "the race of men," or are they "things" of a different kind? Certainly, the Hesiod who is addressed by the Muses as a "shepherd of the wilderness, an ugly disgrace, a mere belly" (26) does not look very much like a "god." And yet, when the Muses endow a ruler, a *basileus*, with the gifts of "wise judgment and gracious word," the members of the assembly will greet him with reverence like a "god" (91), and the same divinity seems to be accorded by his audience to the singer, the *aiodos*, who can dispel a man's *dysphrosyne* (anxiety, sorrow) by his song (93–103).

4. The Hesiodian Vision of Reality

Within the limits of their compact language, the ambiguities of this class cannot be converted into unambiguous statements. They can only be understood historically as phenomena arising from tensions between existential experience, analytical exegesis, and imaginative symbolization at a specific stage of mythospeculation. Understanding the ambiguous symbolism historically, however, does not mean establishing it as a dead object on a point of the time-line, an antique as it were to be preserved for its ornamental value; it means, rather, to participate in its living presence as an event in the quest for truth. Such presence it has indeed, thanks to the intensity of Hesiod's noetic effort in openness to the Beyond; and by virtue of this openness, it not only illuminates the structure of consciousness that we try to explore in its own present but also its past and future as it radiates light on the structure of the more compact myth from which it emerges as well as on the differentiations yet to come. By articulating our mode of understanding the event in this manner we are participating, in fact, in Hesiod's vision of reality as "the things [*ta eonta*] that are, that shall be, and that were before" (38)—the great symbolism that expresses the experienced constancy of structure in the complex of consciousness-reality-language. I shall now trace some of the rays of light cast by the presence of the Beyond in the event on its temporal dimensions of present, past, and future.

Regarding its present: When Hesiod's gods are things and his things are divine, we shall not suspect equivocations caused by the poet's inability to distinguish between gods, men, and things of the external world, but recognize (a) the symbols as ambiguous and (b) the paradoxic tension of consciousness as the source of their ambiguity. Thing-reality and It-reality, although grammatical subjects in propositions, are not entities but tensional poles experienced as mutually participating in the process of reality: The It-reality is the "comprehending" dimension experienced as present in all things, and the things are experienced as "transcending" their existence into the It-reality. All thing-reality, we may say, transcends into It-reality, while the It-reality comprehends all thing-reality. The ambiguities of the Invocations suggest that Hesiod was superbly sensitive to the tension of comprehending-transcending in the paradoxic Whole of reality. The immense manifold of thing-reality carried for him the divine aura of transcending into the comprehending It-reality, and because of their divine aura all things—earth, heaven, sea, stars, mountains, rivers, trees, animals, men—could imaginatively rise to the divine rank, to the rank of the "gods."

Regarding its past, the mythospeculative ambiguities let us become aware of noetic structures in conventionally so-called polytheism that are more difficult to discern on the more compact levels of mythic symbolization. The things have a divine aura. Hence, we shall not be surprised to encounter such thingly subdivisions of divinity as the cosmic gods of heaven and earth, sea and underworld, as the divinely originating elements of earth-water-fire-air, with a quintessential divine ether thrown in, as the chthonic divinities, as theriomorphic and anthropomorphic gods, or the divine psychic forces of love and strife (*eros-eris*).

Inversely, the gods have a thingly aura. They have a thingly enough body to become actors in stories of order and disorder, of benevolent and malevolent, just and unjust, prudential and emotional actions, of suffering and victory; and they even become visible, although their bodies are not composed of the matter that composes things of the external world. About two centuries after Hesiod, this thingly but immaterial body of the gods appears to have become a matter of meditative questioning, as we can gather from the concerned imagery of Xenophanes and Aeschylus. The One God of Xenophanes, although not one of the many gods and "not similar to the mortals either in body [*demas*] or thought" (B 23), seems to have something like a body nevertheless, as he is an "all-seeing, all-knowing, all-hearing" god (B 24), a peculiar body however that "remains always in the same place, not ever moving"—it being improper for a god to move here and there—even when the god without toil (anapeuthe ponoio) is shaking all things "with the thought of his mind" (B 25); and in the *Suppliants* of Aeschylus we meet the god who, from his holy seat, accomplishes his thought "somehow" (empas) without force, for "all that is divine is without toil" (pan aponon daimonion) (96–103). Although the paradoxic issue of immaterial, divine bodies does not cease to be a matter of meditative concern, it will not dissolve under the pressure of differentiation: In the postclassic, imperial contexts we have to note its survival, and even renewed strength, in such symbolisms as the spiritual matter of the Stoics or the Pauline distinction between a carnal and a doxic body. Hesiod's mythospeculation makes us aware of fundamental experiences of reality that require for their expression the language of the gods even when, in the process of differentiation, the many gods are superseded by the One God. The past of experience will not die with differentiation; it is part of the Whole of reality, of "the things that are, that shall be, and that were before."[7]

The god-things participate in an unfinished story of reality. They become transparent for the paradox of consciousness, because Hesiod's mythospeculation does not deal with the gods or things as compactly autonomous entities in autonomous stories (myths), but with their divine and thingly aura as tensional poles in the genetic process of reality as a whole. There is only one reality; this one reality is engaged in its one genetic movement of gods and things toward the one just order of the whole; and if the order is experienced as far from achieved in the present, its imperfection is apprehended as such by a vision of the whole whose order has come to the end of the struggle for its achievement. Dominated by this vision, the gods and things lose their status as compact entities and become participants in the comprehending story of a reality whose struggle for order they have to carry out in genetic time. Not even the Olympian Zeus, as we have seen, is exempt from this participatory struggle but has to seek relief from its unpleasantness through Mnemosyne and the apocalyptically remembering Muses. The experienced tension between the nontensional whole and the

7. References to *Xenophanes* are from the Diels-Kranz edition, *Fragmente der Vorsokratiker*, 7th ed. (Berlin, 1954).

tensional struggle for its realization, the tension between a divine Beyond of time and its temporal Parousia, thus, has differentiated in Hesiod's vision, but the event has not resulted in the creation of correspondingly expressive symbols. The compact symbols become ambiguous, because they have to carry the meanings of a differentiated experience. I am stressing the discrepancy between experience and symbolization in the vision, in order to force attention on the extraordinary difficulties, the hesitations and resistances, that have to be overcome when a thinker fated with the vision—who is a man with a consciousness located in his body, that is located in a bodily society with its compact traditions of symbolization, that is located in a bodily cosmos whose structural evolution culminates in the genesis of mortal humans endowed with consciousness—has to respond to the manifestation in his consciousness of a reality beyond the compact thinglyness of his traditional images of reality—of a Beyond of the gods, a Beyond of the things, a Beyond of the cosmos, of a reality beyond the reality in whose truth he believed to live [he lived?—ES]. The exegetic articulation of this vision and its implications requires participating efforts and takes time. I have already mentioned the more than two centuries it took for a specific detail, for the immaterial body of the gods, to become a matter of concern in the language of Xenophanes and Aeschylus; and even four centuries after Hesiod, in Plato's analytically thorough exploration of the Beyond of being things, the experiential issue of the Hesiodian vision had still to assume the form of a question, of the formidable question "Who is this God?" (*Laws* 713A), this God beyond the gods of the "poets," of Homer and Hesiod.

Because of the discrepancy between experience and symbolization, Hesiod's vision is fraught with a future of experiential and linguistic exegesis that extends into our own present and beyond. The principal events in this process—the creation of the symbols of the Beyond, of the One, of the Whole, of the One God, of Being, of Nothing, of the Fullness, the Pleroma, of divine reality, of the *viae eminentiae* and *negationis*, of affirmative (*kataphatic*) and negative (*apophatic*), of dogmatic and mystic theology—will occupy us in later contexts. For the present, I shall illuminate the meaning of "future" in the vision by concentrating on three such events, distinguished as they are by their closeness to the problems raised by Hesiod himself in his mythospeculation. They are the principle of sufficient reason in the formulation of Leibniz, the symbol of autogenesis as developed by the Neoplatonists, and the meaning of the symbol God as developed by Thomas Aquinas.

I am considering the modern case, the principle of sufficient reason in the formulation of Leibniz, first, because it represents the richest accumulation of Hesiodian "future." As sources for the analysis I am using the late essays on *Les principes de la nature et de la grâce* (*PNG*) and the *Monadologie* (*M*), both written about 1713, circulating among scholars before the death of Leibniz in 1716, but published only posthumously.[8]

The overall problem in the structure of reality raised by Hesiod's vision is the tension between the tensional structures in the temporal process of reality and the nontensional Beyond of the temporal process as a whole. Once the problem is raised, it is exposed to further differentiation in the two directions of a clearer understanding and symbolization of the Beyond and of an improved understanding of the structures internal to the temporal process, as well as to the imaginative elaboration of the symbols that will optimally express the experienced tensions between a Beyond and its Parousia in the spatiotemporal epiphany of structures. During the two and a half millennia between Hesiod and Leibniz, the quest for truth has indeed greatly advanced in both directions, the formative process of experience and symbolization being as always accompanied by the process of deformative reification of the symbols achieved, with the result that, by the time of Leibniz, the god-things of the poet have been formed and deformed into the One-God of the theologians and the things of the mathematicians, physicists, and biologists—with the two poles of the fundamental tension threatening to dissociate into autonomous, unrelated things. In the language of Leibniz, the contingent events of the spatiotemporal process (things, *choses*) have become the concern of the *physiciens*, while the tensional relation of the things to their Beyond, to the One-God of the theologians, having become questionable, is in need of a constructive resymbolization by the efforts of a science called *métaphysique.*

Operating in this mixed medium of vision, formed-deformed symbols, and genuine analysis Leibniz, speaking in the role of the metaphysician, proposes to preserve the unity of the one process

---

8. Quotations from Leibniz are from "Principes de la nature et de la grâce fondés en raison," in *Ausgewaehlte Philosophische Schriften im Originaltext,* by G. W. Leibniz, ed. Herman Schmalenback (Leipzig, 1915), 2:126 f.; cited in the text as PNG.

of the one reality "by using the *grand principe,* commonly little employed, that nothing happens without sufficient reason, i.e., that somebody who is sufficiently familiar with the things [*qui connaîtrait assez les choses*] could not give a reason why it happens this way and not otherwise." If the principle is assumed and accepted (*posé*), there will arise the two questions: (a) "Why is there something rather than nothing? For nothing is simpler and easier than something" and (b) granted that the things have to exist, "Why do they exist as they do and not otherwise[?]" (*PNG*, 7). That sufficient reason for "the existence of the universe is not to be found in the sequence of contingent things, i.e., in the bodies [*corps*] and their representations in the souls [*âmes*]," for in the movement of "matter" one can find neither the reason for movement nor for a specific movement; one would be indefinitely referred back from every present movement to the preceding one as its cause, the basic question always remaining the same. The sufficient reason that has no need of a further reason is to be found in a substance beyond the material sequence (*hors de cette suite des choses contingentes*), a substance that is their cause, in a substance that is "necessary being, carrying the reason of its existence with itself. . . . This ultimate reason of the things is called God" (*PNG,* 8).

In the report of the principle I have endeavored to preserve as faithfully as possible the unwieldy language of the source, this unwieldiness being the historical evidence for the decline from luminosity to intentionality the philosophers' language has suffered by about A.D. 1700. As in the case of Hegel, therefore, the following analytic remarks should be understood, not as a criticism directed against Leibniz, but as an attempt to clarify the mode of the public unconscious prevalent at his time, a mode that the great thinker could not escape while resisting it.

In its fundamental structure the *grand principe* does not differ from Hesiod's vision of reality. Vision, if we use the term in the Platonic sense, is the consciousness of participating in a formative Beyond of thing-reality when partaking of bodily existence in the spatiotemporal process; and vision in this sense animates the argument of Leibniz. It even animates his late essays so strongly that it would be no exaggeration to rank them in the history of vision as a "modern" equivalent to the meditative creation of a medieval saint with empiricist inclinations, to the *Itinerarium mentis in Deum* of Saint Bonaventura. Still, something has happened to the structure of consciousness, the something that causes the symbols, imaginatively arising from the experienced metaxy of existence, to be flattened out into names for objects; the experience of the god-things is still the issue in need of expression, but the language of the gods is slanting toward a language of things, of things that threaten to fall apart in an ungodly manner. Above all, the symbol "God" has suffered badly. The mystery of a reality that is experienced as a meaningful epiphany of structures, the meaning of the whole however not being a given as its Beginning and its End are unknown; the mystery of an It-reality that is experienced as the not-experientiable Beyond of, and nevertheless comprehending Presence in, all thing-reality; the mystery that lets all meaningfully structured stories within the process be experienced as substories of the comprehending story; the mystery of the One-God that evokes Plato's question "Who is this God?"—this mystery has now found a remarkable answer: This God is the "sufficient reason" for a human mind in quest of a causal explanation of things. The ultimate, the sufficient "reason of the things" is a substance or thing that carries the reason of its existence *avec soi*. The *grand mystère* has become the *grand principe,* a piece of information well known to a metaphysician who knows his business, to a connoisseur of *les choses,* to an expert in all of the "things" of whom God is one.

The deformation of the symbol God is not incidental to an otherwise solid analysis, and therefore to be passed over in silence, but symptomatic of a movement in consciousness to transform symbols into concepts by imaginative oblivion of the experiential context from which they arise, a tendency that affects the essay as a whole. The tendency becomes grossly manifest in the remarks on the issue of Something-Nothing, immediately following on the establishment of the principle itself. Once the principle is posited and accepted, Leibniz continues, certain questions have a claim (*droit*) to be asked, the first one being the famous question "Why is there something rather than nothing?" The claim of the question is supported by the experiential argument that "the nothing is simpler and easier than something." While in the vision of an Aeschylus "all that is divine is without toil," the God of Leibniz appears to be a personality who can either cause the universe to exist, an activity which seems to require some effort, or take the easier way of doing nothing at all, a formulation of choice that moves one to wonder why the God who "carries the reason of his existence *avec soi*" should not have chosen the even simpler way out of such decisions by not being the *causa sui,* the simple way of not causing himself to exist in the first place. This extraordinary experiential argument provokes some distancing reflection: As distinguished from Leibniz's God, I for my part find it easier to do something rather than to sit around and do nothing; this finding is complicated, however, by the experience that sometimes when I am doing something I feel I am doing nothing, as when I am engaged in *divertissements* in the Pascalian sense; but furthermore, even when I feel that I am not doing nothing when I am doing something, as for instance just now when I am writing this sentence, my mind will still not be paralyzed into peace by the certainty of doing something rather than nothing, because my action is disturbed by doubts about whether the meditative story I am producing is, within the limits of my human existence, truly the substory of the comprehending story it endeavors to be. By the time of Leibniz, the practice of what may be called conceptually systematizing metaphysics had indeed widely diverged from noetic analysis and its recognition of the mysteries of reality.

The degree of imaginative oblivion involved in the remarks of Leibniz will be more clearly apprehended when they are confronted with the analysis of the same issue in the already-mentioned *Itinerarium mentis in Deum* (*It.*). Saint Bonaventura is aware that Nothing or Non-Being (*non-esse*) is a privation of Being and, since one cannot recognize a privation unless one knows the something of which it is the privation, that the knowledge of Being is primary. "Non-Being [*non-esse*] is the privation of Being [*esse*], it cannot enter the intellect except through Being; Being, however, cannot enter through anything other than itself. . . . Non-Being is intelligible only through Being. . . . That Being is divine Being" (*It.* V, 3). In the saint's analysis there is no primary experience of "contingent things" at all, of the "particular Being, which is restricted Being"; for the recognition of contingency implies the experience of non-contingent actuality; the experienced tension in reality between the divinely formative Beyond and its Parousia in the contingent structures of the spatiotemporal process must not be broken, or the poles of the tension will become autonomous entities. Moreover, the saint is aware of the source of imaginative oblivion, which induces the break nevertheless: "Strange is the blindness of the intellect which does not consider what it sees above all [*prius*] and without which it can know nothing. But just as the eye intent upon the various differences of the colors does not see the light by which it sees the other things [*entia*] and, if it sees it, does not notice it, so our mind's eye, intent upon particular and universal beings [*entia*], does not notice Being itself, which is beyond all genera, though that comes first before the mind and through it all other things" (*It.* V, 4).[9]

The confrontation is instructive. Saint Bonaventura is closer to the compact insights of Hesiod than Leibniz. The god-things, it is true, have differentiated into the One-God who is Being and the things that are Non-Being, but the poles of the tension have not fallen apart. On the contrary, the parallel differentiation of the meditative *intellectus* as the originating site of the experience makes it possible to clarify the togetherness of the poles in the tension: There is no autonomous experience of things; the things are tensionally experienced as "restricted Being"; and there can be no privational experience of things as Non-Being without the experience of the Being of which it is a privation. The meditative symbols of the saint, moving within the differentiated context of Platonic and Christian tradition, express equivalently the poet's divine aura of things and thingly aura of the gods. However, while Hesiod's language is burdened with the ambiguities of an emergent differentiation, Saint Bonaventura's language has a defensive touch induced by a sense of the deformative cracks that threaten the achieved formations and will widen in the future. The radical distinction of Being and Non-Being, replacing the Platonic symbolism of a formative Beyond and its Parousia in formed reality, stresses the formative eminence of the Beyond in the experienced tension of reality so strongly that it acquires an ontic monopoly that cannot be sustained in the course of the analysis; the "Non-Being" cannot avoid becoming synonymous with "restricted Being"; and "restricted Being," while not the *ipsum esse* of Being, is some sort of Being after all. The new ambiguity, it appears, must be read as the consequence of an attempt to ward off a threatening disruption of the paradox of consciousness: A publicly noticeable inclination to identify the thing-reality with Being is compensated by according

9. The quotations from the *Itinerarium* are Voegelin's translations from the Latin text in *Works of Saint Bonaventure,* ed. Philotheus Boehner, O.F.M., and Sr. M. Frances Laughlin, S.I.M.C., vol. 2, *Itinerarium mentis in Deum* (New York, 1956), 82.

the monopoly of Being to the comprehending reality. What the saint wants to prevent is the potential transformation of the thing-reality into Being and, correspondingly, of the divine Being into Non-Being, i.e., the potential deformation that has become actual in the development of the public unconscious from the eighteenth to the twentieth century. This reading is confirmed by Saint Bonaventura's analysis of the potential of deformation in the *intellectus,* in the Nous. The *intellectus* is exposed to the disease of blindness, to the *caecitas intellectus,* breaking out in the pathological phenomena of imaginative oblivion.

§4. Remembrance of Reality*

Within the limits of their own language, the ambiguities of this type cannot be converted into unambiguous statements. They can only be understood historically as phenomena arising from tensions between existential experience, analytical exegesis, and imaginative symbolization at a specific stage of mythospeculation. The dominant symbols themselves, however, although they cause the ambiguities by their want of analytical articulation, are eminently luminous. In fact, the Hesiodian verse on the "things" that are, that will be, and that were before is so sensitive a response to the mystery of divine formation in all reality that it has become something like a catalytic constant in the symbolization of the experience through millennia of differentiation. A few representative examples will illuminate the millennial function of the symbolism.

1. *From the Seer to the Singer (Homer-Hesiod)—* Ta Eonta

The full temporal range of the symbolism cannot be determined with certainty, because its appearance in the *Theogony* is already an event in the process of differentiation. The summary symbolization of reality as the things that are, that will be, and that were before, in

*Voegelin was not able to complete his expansion of the preceding section, "Hesiod's Mnemosyne." Therefore, he did not provide the appropriate transition that would remove the repetition here of two sentences from the beginning of "The Hesiodian Vision of Reality." For the "ambiguities" referred to in the repetition here of those sentences, the reader can refresh his memory by glancing again at Voegelin's discussion of "certain problems of symbolization" connected with Hesiod's compact language, pages 90–92. Cf. also "Quod Deus Dictur" in *CW,* 12:376–94.

Theogony v. 38, is to be found in the presumably earlier Homeric context, in *Iliad* I, 70; and whether it is original with Homer, or whether it has a long prehistory, we do not know because of the lack of sources. We can only discern the differentiating change of meaning that has occurred in the transition from Homer to Hesiod.

Although in the Homeric context the *eonta* are no more objects of the external world than in the Hesiodian, they are still concrete events, experienced as resulting from a conflict between divinely willed order and human actions violating the order. The pestilence inflicted upon the Achaeans by Apollo has to be explained as to its cause, and the means to bring the disaster to an end must be revealed. The persons who know about such things, and can be consulted on the occasion, are characterized variously as seer (*mantis*), or priest (*hieros*), or reader of dreams (*oneiropolos*), or diviner (*oionopolos*) (*Iliad* I, 62–63, 69). The choice falls on Calchas, who has previously given proof of being endowed by Apollo with the art of divination (*mantosyne*) (*Iliad* I, 71–72). While in the Homeric passage, thus, the "things" still are a variegated manifold of events, suspected by the afflicted to be of an existentially tensional nature, and while the ability to penetrate the opaque events is distributed over a variety of mantic specialists, Hesiod has discerned the divine presence as formatively moving in all of the "things," comprising the whole evolutionary range of reality from earth and heaven to the just order of gods and men, and has concentrated the ability to reveal this truth of reality in the person of the remembering *aiodos*, the singer for everyman.

2. *The Knowing Man (Parmenides)*—To Eon

The efforts to cope with the Hesiodian insight, to further articulate the insufficiently differentiated Beyond, and thereby to dissolve the ambiguities, can be traced through the history of Hellenic poetry and philosophy. A representative instance is the Parmenidean attack on the Homeric-Hesiodian symbolism of the "things." If the experience of the Beyond was to be adequately expressed, it could not be classified as one of the "things," of *ta eonta*, in which it was revealed as a formative presence. In Parmenides we have to note, therefore, the transition from the plural *ta eonta* to the singular *to eon*. The "being" that is compactly predicated of all being "things" becomes for him the "Being" that is none of the "things." Against

Hesiod, as well as against the "double-heads" (*dikranoi*) who cannot find their way out of the ambiguities, he insists that this Being in the singular has not come into being, or it would not "be"; this Being is never a Was nor ever a Will-be, but is always in its Now (*nyn*), altogether as a Whole, a One, a Continuous or Coherent (*syneches*) (Parm. B 8, 5–6). The divine Beyond as the eternal *Now*, as the Augustinian *nunc*, the structure that I have symbolized as the flux of divine presence, begins to become articulate.

The existential excitement of the discovery must have been intense, for Parmenides was moved by it to appropriate the symbol "being" so radically for the Beyond that the newly differentiated Being, *to eon* in the singular, let the ontic status of *ta eonta*, of the being things, become questionable. Fortunately, the thinker's self-analysis of the conscious-unconscious movement that caused the radical appropriation has been preserved. Parmenides insists that "thinking [*noein*] and the thought [*noema*] that Is (is)" are one and the same, for there is no thinking (*noein*) "without the being [*to eon*] in which it is a spoken symbol [*pephatismenon*]" (Parm. B 8, 34–36). As a consequence of this identification, all the language "the mortals have established, believing it to be true, such as becoming and perishing, being and not-being" is no more than a "name" (*onoma*) (Parm. B 8, 38–41). Although the Parmenidean language is compact, we can discern that its thinker has become conscious of the paradox of consciousness, of the tension between intentionality and luminosity, between thing-reality and It-reality, as well as of the complex of consciousness-reality-language in its integrality. He is aware that his own thinking partakes of the Being to which the language of *ta eonta* refers as if it were no more than an object given to a subject. The Being he has differentiated is the structure of the It-reality in consciousness. In fact, one of his translators, Kathleen Freeman, felt obliged to render the previously quoted passage as: "To think is the same as the thought that It Is."

In the light of this understanding we have to read the famous, succinct Fragment B 3: "For the same is thinking [*noein*] and being [*einai*]." The thinker has become the speaker of the It- reality with such self-assertive assurance that the balance of consciousness is disturbed. That he also is the speaker of a bodily located consciousness, of the human being known as Parmenides, becomes problematic. The excitement to have discovered the truth that will overcome the ambiguities of *ta eonta* has carried the thinker into a new ambiguity on the differentiated level of *to eon*. The structure of the movement, from ambiguity to ambiguity, is the same that we have to observe in the Hegelian movement of thought. The identification of thinking and being inevitably recalls the equally famous Hegelian identification in the *Vorrede* to the *Philosophie des Rechts:* "Was vernuenftig ist, das ist wirklich; was wirklich ist, das ist vernuenftig" ("What is reasonable, is real; what is real is reasonable"). Unfortunately, what is unreasonable is also real.[10]

3. The Philosopher (Plato)—To Pan

In his self-understanding, Parmenides speaks of himself as the "knowing man" (*eidos phos*) (B 1, 3). Guided by the Heliconian maidens, he finds his way to "the goddess" who reveals to him the truth of Being in *oratio directa* (B 1). The excitement that carried the "knowing man" from assertive to self-assertive symbolization provoked the balancing resistance of the "philosopher," of the Socrates-Plato who knows that he does not know and, even more important, who knows why he does not know.

In the *Timaeus*, Plato developed the differentiated context of experience and symbolization into which the Hesiodian and Parmenidean concern with the being things, with *ta eonta*, has to be placed. The dominant symbol expressing the experience of reality now shifts from *to eon* to *to pan*, to the All (27c). Other synonyms are admitted: "the whole [*pas*] Cosmos or Uranos"—or "any other name by which it prefers to be called" (28b). This All is a "Living Being" (*zoon*), comprising all other living beings, including gods and men, within it. As a Living Being it consists of an intelligible structure, the *Nous*, formatively invested in a life force, the Psyche, which in its turn is embodied in materials accessible to sense perception, in the Soma. The complex of Nous–in Psyche–in Soma symbolizes the structure of cosmic reality, regarding the comprehending All as well as its parts (30b).

The quest for truth is concerned with the genesis and structure of the All, and above all with the question whether it is created or uncreated (28c). The change in the dominant symbol, thus, is

10. References to Parmenides are to the Diels-Kranz edition cited in note 7 above. For the Parmenides passages (B8) translated by Freeman and quoted here, see Kathleen Freeman, *Ancilla to the Pre-Socratic Philosophers* (Oxford, 1952), 44. For the Hegel quotation, see Hegel, *Philosophie des Rechts*, vol. 7 of the Jubilee edition, ed. Herman Glockner (Stuttgart, 1964), 33.

accompanied by a transition from Hesiod's biologically successive generations to a demiurgic, creational act. Plato experiences his Cosmos, the All, as an imposition of order (*taxis*) on a state of primordial disorder (*ataxia*), as an intelligible work of ordering craftsmanship operating on disorderly materials (30A). Accordingly, the Cosmos, *to pan*, can neither be a biological unfolding of compact *ta eonta*, nor a radically differentiated *to eon*, but has to consist of something that is always being (*to on aei*) and never has genesis, together with a something else that is always becoming (*to gignonenon aei*) and never has being (27D–28A). It is a composite of nongenetic being and non-being genesis, both components characterized by the adverb *aei* as lasting or everlasting. Synonymously with the everlasting components "being" and "genesis," Plato uses the Same and the Other, resuming the symbols from his analysis of the fundamental categories of reality in the *Sophist*.

The matter becomes linguistically further complicated when Plato uses *ousia* as a synonym for *to on aei*, for the "being" that is the opposite of "genesis" (29C), but then classifies both "being" and "genesis" as "kinds of being," as *ousias eidos* (35A). Moreover, since the All is not a static entity but a something in continuous process of formation, Plato places between (*en meso*) the two kinds of being a third kind, the Psyche. This third kind of being is composed of the Same and the Other, the two opposed kinds of "being" forced together by a third force, again called "being" (*ousia*). This third, composite kind of being is meant to preserve the flow of order between the opposites "being" and "genesis" (35A ff.). To top it off, the All is something like a being thing in the Hesiodian sense after all, as it is supposed to be a "god" (34B). Obviously, the linguistic means are not quite sufficient to meet the analytical demands. The complicated experience of reality will not let itself be covered by a simple meaning of the symbol "being." We have to explore the Platonic symbolization a step further, in order to find what has become of *ta eonta*.

The new difficulties surrounding the symbol "being" arise from the advance in the articulation of meditative consciousness. Plato's resistance traces the ambiguities of language to their source in the ambiguity of a reality that reveals its truth in consciousness, to their source in what we have called the paradox of consciousness governing the complex of consciousness-reality-language. The resistance is carried by the insight that our thinking in the mode of "things" is comprehended as an event by a something, *to pan*, that is not a thing like the things of sense perception that come and go, and yet partakes of such thingness, for the All experienced as the Cosmos with its Uranos of celestial bodies is visible, is accessible to sense perception. The All is neither being nor not-being because it is both, the order between the opposites being persuasively mediated by the process of the psychic reality "between" (*en meso*) being and genesis. The "between" existence of consciousness, then, is part of the metaxic structure of the Cosmos. And the metaxic structure of the Cosmos, finally, reveals itself as its truth through the analysis of the quest for the truth of order in the "philosopher's" personal existence that is an event in the Cosmos. There is no truth of reality other than the reality of the truth manifesting itself in the quest. We are close to the differentiation of consciousness that we discerned as the background in the symbolism of the biblical book of Genesis.

While in the biblical story the structure of consciousness remains in the background, it moves into the foreground of exploration in the "philosopher's" analysis. The pneumatic, irruptive experiences, which speak the language of the gods, are taken for granted; the primary concern is with the noetic, searching experiences that, as they are moving toward a critically balanced language of reality, lead to more suitable symbolizations of divinity. His is the *fides quaerens intellectum*. Concretely, Plato's *fides* is of a Cosmos that reveals its divinity through the presence of a divine, intelligible order. The Platonic Cosmos is a "god." Under this aspect, the *fides* is quite close in its structure to the Hesiodian *eonta*. Still, it advances decisively beyond them as it expresses the experience of a Whole that comprehends the *eonta*. In the *fides* of the Cosmos, the Hesiodian *eonta* have absorbed the Parmenidean *to eon*; the manifold of the particular *eonta* has become their *to pan*. When such a symbol emerges in consciousness from the process of reality, it becomes the philosopher's task to explore it analytically. As Plato formulated the task: "What we are obliged to inquire [*skepteon*] first," what in all cases (*peri pantos*) has to be explored "to begin with" (*en arche*), is the question whether the something symbolized has a genetic beginning or whether it has "a beginning from some beginning" (28B). Whether the Cosmos has a beginning, or whether it is lasting in eternity, thus, is a problem that arises both from the pneumatic vision of a comprehending Whole and from the reality of the obligatory question in the philosopher's noetic existence.

Plato's answer to the question that has agitated the history of theology and philosophy through the millennia is rendered in due paradoxic form. Since the Cosmos has a visible Soma, and what is visible partakes of genesis, the Cosmos has to be generated (*genonen*) (28B). The Cosmos has a beginning. Since the Cosmos, however, also has an intelligible, everlasting structure, and as it is the comprehending (*perilabon*) Whole of all things, the beginning is not to be found on the genetic level of finite things (30C–D); the "cause," the *aition* of the Cosmos (28C), is not a matter of causality among things of the external world. The *aition* of the Cosmos, its "beginning," is a paradigmatic order (*paradeigma*) designed by a divine Demiourgos and, when found good by him by the standard of his own unenvious goodness, applied to the formation of the genetic Cosmos. The visible Cosmos, then, is an *eikon*, an image of the eternal paradigm. Moreover, in order to bring the genetic image as close as possible to the eternal paradigm in its character of eternity, the Demiourgos endowed the image, through the creation of the celestial bodies and their mathematically determined movements, with a moving image of eternity, with the *eikon* of eternity that is called Time, this image of eternity itself being an eternal image (*aionios eikon*) (37D).

I have no more than intimated the *Timaeus* story of the Beginning, for it is well known as to its letter. What I want to bring to attention is its spirit, i.e., the Platonic struggle to advance the symbolization of existential consciousness. In tracing this struggle, we have to note the scattering of the symbol "eternal" (*aionios*) over the structural manifold of consciousness, paralleling the previously analyzed scattering of the symbol "being." Not only the paradigm is eternal, but its visible image, the Cosmos, is eternal, too (barring the hypothetical dissolution of the Uranos, 38B); not only the eternity of the paradigm is eternal, but also Time, the image of this eternity; and finally, the primordial, disorderly something on which the paradigm is imposed, the something that is neither paradigmatically eternal nor accessible to sense perception but only to a dreamlike awareness, precedes the imposition of paradigmatic order. Plato feels obliged, therefore, to add to the initially distinguished kinds of being, i.e., to being and genesis, a third kind of being (*ousias eidos*), called *chora*, Space. The triad of Being-Becoming-Space is "being" (*on te kai choran kai genesin einai*), before even Uranos has "become" (*genesthai*) (52D).

§5. Plato's *Timaeus*

One could expound on the language of the *Timaeus* and its literalist
inconsistencies, as well as on the controversies about the internal
logic and construction of the dialogue based on their observation,
but the examples given should be sufficient to make the point at
issue clear. Plato is struggling for a language that will optimally express the analytical movements of existential consciousness within
the limits of a *fides* of the Cosmos. I shall try to formulate some of
the important results of this struggle.

1. The Tensional Symbols

The symbols "being" and "eternal" are not scattered at random
over concepts defining objects of the external world but appear as
distinguishing attributes of symbols that emerge in groups as the in-
dicators of analytical movements in existential consciousness. The
symbols distinguished by such specific attributions of existence
and constancy, i.e., such symbols as Taxis, Ataxia, Being, Genesis,
Paradigm, Eikon, Eternity, Time, derive their meaning from their
membership in the tensional complexes of Taxis-Ataxia, Being-
Becoming, Paradigm-Eikon, Eternity-Time; they would lose their
meaning if the complexes were fragmented and their parts hypostatized into intentionalist entities. Moreover, these dyadic complexes
themselves, which express tensions experienced in reality, do not
refer to ultimate "things" either. For, as we have noted, they have
a tendency to expand into such triadic complexes as Nous-Psyche-
Soma, or Being-Genesis-Space, not to mention the triad of Same-
Other-Being resumed from the *Sophist.* If then we consider that on
one occasion the Psyche is intercalated as a "third kind of being"
between Being and Becoming, while on another occasion the *chora*
appears as the "third kind of being" added to Being and Becoming,
we might arrive at tetradic complexes. And finally, we have to
remember the complex of Beginning-Beyond-End whose meaning
pervades the other complexes, although the relations among the
various complexes are not made explicitly thematic. What thus
emerges from the *Timaeus* is the understanding of complexes of
symbols as the expressive constants in the movements of noetic
consciousness, as well as the problem of the relations among these
complexes in the comprehending structure of consciousness.

2. *The Tensions and Their Poles*

The complex symbolisms express the poles of tensions experienced in reality as well as the tensions themselves. The tensional character of the experiences causes the linguistic difficulties we had to observe. The ever-being being is "being," but its opposite, the never-being genesis, has to be "being," too; the eternal eternity is "eternal," but the same is true of the noneternal time. Reality is experienced as a tensional oneness in which the poles of the tension carry different weights of reality, while the tension between the poles has its own weight of constancy. Some kinds of being appear to be more being than others, and some kinds of eternity more eternal than other kinds, while a comprehending consciousness experiences these very differences of degree as constants to be distinguished by the attributes "being" and "eternal." Hence, the linguistic ambiguities of this type are not caused by some negligence in Plato's thought or writing. Plato was well aware of them and traced them to the paradox that governs the complex of consciousness-reality-language. The linguistic ambiguities become the unambiguous paradox in Plato's reformulation of the Hesiodian-Parmenidean problem of *ta eonta* under the conditions of the new experience of *to pan* (37C–38B). If the Cosmos, *to pan*, consists of both Being and Becoming, the language of "being" and "becoming" is or becomes paradoxic. There was no time, Plato insists, before the generation of time as the moving, eternal image of eternity. Hence, the time language of "was" or "shall be" is used wrongly when it is applied to eternal being (*ten aidion ousian*), even if we habitually use it without being aware of the incorrectness; the only proper term when speaking of eternal being would be "is" (*esti*); "was" and "shall be" can be properly applied only to sensually perceived genesis as it proceeds in time. Moreover, the same argument governs the inverse relation in the tension of the *to pan*. Again without being aware of the incorrect habit, we say something "becomes (*is* become)" (*einai gegonos*), or something "*is* becoming" (*einai gignomenon*), or "*is* about to become" (*einai genesomenon*); or in speaking of something non-being (*me on*) we habitually say that it "is" non-being. In reflective distance Plato, thus, is conscious of the paradox of consciousness, of the structures of thing-reality and It-reality that govern the language of reality. One can raise the potential consequence of the paradox, the potential of deforming the language of reality through habitual unconsciousness, as well as the paradox itself, to the level of consciousness in reflective distance, as Plato does in this masterly page, but one cannot escape from it short of creating a language beyond reality and its paradox. Plato refused to discuss the matter further in this context (38B), but he certainly did not attempt to transcend the paradox linguistically. Hegel, as we shall see, when faced with the paradoxic structure of language, tried to master the problem by inventing a language that would out-comprehend the comprehending paradox.

3. The Levels of Paradoxic Language—The Constant and the Super-Constant

In the course of his noetic analysis Plato has encountered the difficulties of symbolization a philosopher has to overcome when he wants to speak unambiguously of the paradox governing reality while using the medium of language that is itself part of the reality governed by the paradox. On a first level of meaning, the symbols expressing the poles of tensional experiences do not only radiate their luminosity, but also carry the intentionalist mode of reference and can, therefore, induce the misconception of the poles as "being things," a misconception that causes their later deformation into "metaphysical" entities. To avert such a misconception, the thinker must remain aware that the symbolized poles appear in complexes of symbols and that only the integral complex validly expresses the truth of the generating tension. If he is acutely aware of this problem, he will be moved to create a second level of language that will stress the residing of the truth in the tensional complex rather than in the poles taken singly. In the Platonic case, this awareness and movement lead to the scattering of the symbols "being" and "eternal" over the tensional poles which, on the first level, were distinguished as Being and Becoming, Being and Not-Being, Eternity and Time. Through the scattering of attributes the reality of the tension is weighted to match the reality of its poles. If such a second level of language is introduced, however, the tensional complexes could be "psychologically" misconstrued as the ultimate entities to which the symbols "being" and "eternal" apply, reducing the relative weights of reality that have become luminous in the poles of the tension. The misunderstanding could perhaps lead to a psychology of "archetypes." Yet even if one tries to avoid

Plato's equivocational language and its potential for deformation, as I have tried to do by using on the second level the language of "constants" of experience and symbolization, the problem will not quite dissolve, because the supposed "constants" turn out to be not altogether constant. We had to observe the medley of dyadic, triadic, and tetradic complexes and their relations, as well as the changes in the dominant symbols from *ta eonta* to *to eon* to *to pan*. The "constants" appear to point beyond themselves toward a super-constant governing the intelligible relations among the constants as well as the intelligible advances of experience and symbolization in the process of reality. A third level of language, reflectively distancing the structure of tensions and poles, seems to be required. When Plato encountered these problems of a super-constant and of a third, reflectively distancing language, he tried to resolve them through the symbolism of the Cosmos, or the *to pan*, "or whatever it prefers to be called."

4. The One Cosmos

When the exploration of tensional experiences has become so broad, and analytically so penetrating, that the problem of the super-constant imposes itself, the paradox of thing-reality and It-reality becomes acutely conscious. The tensions experienced and symbolized cannot be classified as "things," as individuals of a species "tension," for such a construction would destroy their intelligible meaning as diversified movements in the one quest for truth; the construction would lead to the dead end of some variety of "structuralism," whether binary or arithmetically more generous. If the mistake is avoided, as it is by Plato, and the experienced tensions are recognized as diversifications of the fundamental tension in reality and its truth, however, the potential of deformative hypostatization recurs on the level of this insight in the form of the question whether there is only one real "world," or more than one, or perhaps an infinite number of "worlds." Is the Cosmos an individual of the species "cosmos," or is there only one Cosmos, and if so, why? Plato's answer to the question is paradoxic but not ambiguous. Although the Cosmos is accessible to sense perception (*aisthesis*), it is not a member of a class of individual "things." It is experienced as the image (*eikon*) of the paradigmatic *to pan*, of the divinely designed comprehending (*periechon*) reality of all living beings. The symbol *"periechon"* is to be taken seriously; it must not be rendered as "comprehensive" in the sense of embracing a lot of reality, while leaving another lot outside, but as indeed "comprehending" all of reality. The paradigm of the *zoon*, of the living order of reality, is One; if there were a second Cosmos, there would have to be another paradigm comprehending the two "worlds." The phantasy of multiple "worlds" is incompatible with the experience of the It-reality, and, inversely, a reality that engenders a consciousness of itself both intentional and luminous can be only One. This oneness of the One pertains, not to one of the poles of a tensional constant, or even of the super-constant, but to the Cosmos in the sense of the tensional process of reality. Plato stresses the importance of this point by creating a new symbolism for expressing the experience. The Cosmos is *monogenes*. The symbol *monogenes* will be rendered only inadequately by such phrases as unique, or one-of-its-kind, or only-born, as they still imply a numerical oneness; the oneness intended is not numerical, but the experienced oneness of existential tension, the tension of a *periechon* that is all of the "things" while comprehending them in the intelligible whole of its process. The Cosmos as the *monogenes* is not a "thing" but the visible (*aisthetos*) god generated in the image (*eikon*) of the intelligible (*noetos*) god, the intelligible god not being the Demiourgos but the noetic paradigm (92C). The linguistic difficulties in expressing the experience of this tensional oneness were so great that Plato was forced to coin a new word for its adequate characterization, the word *monosis* (31B). The Cosmos has been generated *monogenes* in order to make it image most perfectly the *monosis* of the divine *paradigm* (31B). Monogenesis as the image of Monosis thus parallels the symbolization of Time as the image of Eternity.

5. *Monosis and Monogenesis*

The symbol *"monosis"* has not been preserved in the history of philosophy. It disappeared under the impact of the related movements of spiritual revolt and imperial expansion that occurred in the following centuries. The noetic analysis of the paradox conducted within the *fides* of the divine Cosmos was obscured when the *fides* of cosmic order itself was shaken by a state of alienation induced by the disordering effect of the events that let the cosmos become a synonym for the *orbis terrarum* to be conquered, and when the experiential emphasis shifted toward the divinity that, by its grace, would save man from a "world" that had become a synonym for disordered existence. The paradoxic *to pan* as the carrier of the attribute One had to contend with such new dominant symbols as the dyad of One God–One World, or the ecumenically activist triad of One God–One World–One Empire. The story of reality had to be retold, incorporating the historic events and their symbolization, and the work of noetic penetration had to be resumed on this vastly more complicated scene of experience and symbolization. Still, while the *monosis* disappeared in the process, its genetic *eikon*, the symbol *monogenes*, survived: The Gospel of John made it the attribute of the Son of God (1:14, 18; 3:16, 18). But these are matters to be considered in more detail in later parts of the analysis.

6. *The Beyond and Its Parousia*

The wandering of the symbol *"monogenes"* from the Cosmos to the Christ reveals the movement of experiential emphasis from the God who creates the order of the Cosmos to the God who saves from its disorder. While Plato could not foresee the forms the movement would concretely assume in the events after his death, he was conscious of its presence in his own quest for truth as well as of the problems its presence created for the language of the gods. We must trace his ironically tentative treatment of these problems, because on some points his formulations are analytically more successful than the later attempts of the Christian theologians to find the *intellectus* of their *fides*.

Plato has understood the mystery of the Beyond and its Parousia. The experiences of divine, formative presence are events in the metaxy of existence, and the symbols engendered by the Parousia express divine reality as an irruption of ordering force from the Beyond into the existential struggle for order. Hence, the symbols can illuminate the mysterious structure of existential reality as a tension tending toward an order beyond itself, and they can articulate the mysterious experience of an ordering Beyond of experience irrupting into experienced presence; but the illuminating articulation cannot make the mystery of the Beyond and its Parousia less mysterious. The imaginative language of the gods can express the presence of a reality beyond its presence, but the symbolized Parousia of the Beyond does not dissolve the Beyond into its Parousia in the experienced tension. Even when the divine Beyond reveals itself in its formative presence, it remains the unrevealed divine reality beyond its revelation. At a more compact stage of experience and symbolization, the language of the gods can cope with this structure of the mystery by endowing one of the many gods experienced as present with the representation of divine reality beyond the gods. In the Egyptian Amon Hymns of the thirteenth century B.C., for instance, the god "Amon" was entrusted with this representative function; the same ambiguous status of compact presence and differentiated nonpresence can still be discerned in the Hebrew "Yahweh," whose name appears in the newly discovered Ebla texts as that of one of the many gods of the Near Eastern pantheon; and in Hesiod's elaborate invocations of the Muses we could follow in detail the poet's efforts to symbolize the stratification of the mystery from an Olympian to a Jovian to a theogonic Beyond in the language of the many gods.

7. *The Oneness of Divine Reality and the One God*

A further complication in the truth of the mystery, accompanied by a new need for discretion, makes itself felt when the divinely revelatory and humanly questing process in the metaxy reaches the point of differentiation at which the oneness of divine reality becomes noetically thematic as it does in Plato's *fides* of the Cosmos. I have stressed that the *monosis* of the Cosmos does not signify a numerical oneness but symbolizes the revelation of the tensional oneness in reality. When the paradox of thing-reality and It-reality that governs the complex of consciousness-reality-language has become sufficiently differentiated, the divine force ordering the oneness of tensional existence reveals itself as One. A Cosmos experienced as the *periechon* of all living beings reveals a oneness of divine reality as its ground (*aition*), however manifold its presence, its Parousia, might be experienced. But can this oneness of divine reality, revealed by the *fides* of the one, comprehending Cosmos, be truly symbolized by a numerically One God who, as a "new god," enters into competition with the many gods of the more compact language of the gods? Can the problem indeed be reduced to the generally accepted, numerical cliché of "monotheism" and "polytheism"? Would the numerical cliché not reduce the one God to the same rank as his more compact, many confrères and expose him to the same noetic questioning of his divinity as the others? Would he be exempt from the mystery of the Beyond and its Parousia in the metaxy, or would he be no more than a Parousia of the truly One beyond the one god? These are the questions encountered by Plato, as they were encountered by his Jewish, Christian, and Islamic successors who found it necessary to create the symbols of a tetragrammatic God beyond the personal God, or of an *En Soph*, or an *Ungrund*, or a *Gottheit* beyond the God of dogmatic theology.

8. The One God and the Many Gods

Such sensitivity of human response to the mystery of divine revelation never was, and still is not, popular with dogmatic thinkers who want their *fides* to speak the language of the compact, personal gods. But the mystery resists and persists. The noetic thinker, who is conscious of this persistence, knows that even the *fides* of the One God does not put an end to his quest for the truly One in a reality that has to tell a story of tension and movement. For a Plato, therefore, the experienced reality of the continuing quest moves all symbols of divinity into a reflective distance in which the awe inspired by the mystery of divine revelation blends with a skeptical detachment aroused by its all-too-human symbolization. On the one hand, the symbolization of the differentiated divine Beyond as One God would burden the symbol with the very compactness of the many gods that the differentiation tends to overcome; on the other hand, the insight into this difficulty lets the many gods appear in their dignity as experientially diversified representatives of the divine One. Far from relegating the many gods to falsehood and oblivion, the insight elevates them, as representative revelations of the divine One, to the same rank as the symbol One God, although on a lesser level of noetic clarity. From the distancing reflections, thus, there seems to emerge a historical field of revelatory tension. In this field, all the gods have to live under the pressure of a divine Beyond that endows them with their divine life while threatening to let them die from their compactness. We remember the Hesiodian Muses who have to remember the gods of their divinity. This tensional pressure appears to be a constant in the history of revelation. Neither will the gods disappear, nor will the Beyond let them live in peace. Compactness and differentiation, then, would not be simply historical stages of consciousness, the one succeeding the other in time, but poles of a tensional process in which the revelation of the Beyond has to overcome progressively a hard core of compact resistance without ever dissolving it completely. Plato was conscious of this hard core and tried to find its experiential source in the structure of existence.

9. The Disorder of Things—Space

The general tone for Plato's language of the gods is set by the quip: "but as for us men, largely as we partake of the accidental and the random, so does our speech" (34C). The ironic aside refers us back to the source of resistant compactness in the metaxic structure of the cosmos, i.e., to existence in the tension of order-disorder. In Plato's Cosmos we live in an order of things that is flawed by the disorder of the accidental and the random, not to mention the Hesiodian list of miseries afflicting the existence of man. The Cosmos is luminous for the paradox of imperfection-perfection, of an order in movement toward order. Moreover, man is not only conscious of the paradox, not only does he "know" about it, he partakes of it inasmuch as the bodily located psyche called man is one of the "things" in the cosmic order of things. He participates in the disorder of things as much as in their order. The paradox of order-disorder, thus, seems to attach to existence in the mode of thingness. But if it attaches to thingness, can there be an order of "things" free of disorder? Or would the establishment of true order require the abolition of "things"? But if the "things" were abolished, what would there remain to be in order or disorder? Plato raises these questions, not in order to dispose of them with clever answers, but in order to raise the paradox of thing-reality and It-reality to full consciousness.

The questions are serious, because the experience of thing-reality cannot be talked away: "We affirm as somehow necessary that all that is has to be in some spot [topos] or to occupy some place [chora]; and that whatever is neither on earth nor anywhere in the heaven [ouranos] is not at all" (52B). There is something in the structure of consciousness-reality-language that forces us to think in the mode of thingness, this something being the third, or fourth, "kind of being," i.e, the chora, Space. This "kind of being" is not itself identifiable as a "thing," either by sense perception or by the Nous; it is the "unsensed" something, experienced as in a dream, behind all formed thingness. The dreamlike sense of the unsensed *chora,* of Space, appears to impose on all reality, as well as on all thought of reality, the mode of thingness. It almost sounds as if the paradigmatic Cosmos, when embodied in the medium of Space, had to submit to a thingness from whose disorder there is no escape into true order.

10. The Meditative Procedure

The assumption is tempting but it must be dismissed as a grave deformation of Plato's analysis. It would transform luminous symbols, as they emerge from tensional experiences, into intentionalist concepts referring to objects. The transformation would destroy the paradoxic structure of reality, thought, and language that Plato wants to clarify by participating in its diversification. In order to understand the meaning of the symbols, we have to follow him on the way he traces through the diversified manifold of tensions in his one quest for truth. The truth of the quest is not a true doctrine resulting from an intentionalist investigation of objects, but a balanced state of existence, formed in reflective distance to the process of meditative wandering through the paradoxic manifold of tensions. The fragmentation of the process into its anamnetic steps would deliver nothing but doctrinal deformations of reality, such as the assumption just dismissed. Only the process comprehending the steps, when moved into reflective distance, will let the truth of existence become luminous by letting the symbols illuminate one another. I shall try to present Plato's procedure for the case of the passage on the things in Space (52B).

11. The Mutual Illumination of Symbols—Things and Non-Things

The "beings" of the passage in question include the gods. All of the "beings" are burdened "necessarily" with the imagery of spatial location in relation to a human consciousness that is located bodily between "heaven" and "earth." The observation does not differ substantially from the initial formulation we attempted in our own analysis of the structure of thing-reality in consciousness. But why should we have to think in the mode of thing-reality, if a considerable number of the "things" we are talking about obviously are not objects in Space? Plato's answer: The "things" are in Space because the Cosmos *has* Space.

With this answer we are entering the process of mutual illumination among the symbols emerging in the course of the quest for truth. For the Cosmos is one of the "things" that is not an object in Space. The experience of the Cosmos as the *periechon* of all things, as their *to pan*, or "whatever it prefers to be called," is carefully symbolized as a non-thing through the *monosis* of its paradigm as well as the *monogenesis* of its image; it is the It-reality comprehending the "things." Although its structural status is that of the comprehending It-reality, this Cosmos is supposed to *have* "body" or "space," as it does in the symbolizations of its integral structure by either the triad of Nous–in Psyche–in Soma or that of Being-Becoming-Space. But then again, although the non-thing Space is an integral part of the non-thing Cosmos, it is explicitly not the same "kind" of non-thing as its fellow parts, i.e., the noetically forming Being and the noetically formed Becoming. As a consequence of this difference, will Space then not be after all some sort of pre-bodily material, introducing problems of "realization," when the noetic paradigm is applied to its *monogenes* image?

But the dyadic symbolism of Paradigm-Eikon, far from supporting this construction, will rather illuminate a further facet of the complicated symbol Space. For the imaging Cosmos has Space because it images the Space that is an integral part of the paradigmatic Cosmos. The paradigm is not put into Space, but Space is in the paradigm. If then one were to ask wherein precisely the difference between the paradigmatic and the eikonic Cosmos should consist (a part of the general question whether the "ideas" are "things" *in re* or *ante rem*), Plato would answer that neither of the two is a "thing" and refer the questioner to the emergence of the dyadic symbolism from the question of the Beginning, from the search for the *aition* of the Cosmos.

The symbolized experience of the Beginning, then, would point further to the comprehending symbolism of a Beyond, the *epekeina*, of the cosmic reality in which the quest for the truth of its order is an event. The quest for truth as an event in cosmic reality appears to be ultimately the "place" at which reality reveals itself in its structural complexity of thing-reality and It-reality. The event of the quest is the "place" at which the bodily located consciousness of man experiences itself both in its thingly existence, i.e., as moving in the thingly tensions of order-disorder, and in its visionary existence, as a movement toward an unflawed order beyond the order that is flawed by the disorder of thingness. But what does the ultimacy of the "place" mean, if the event reveals itself as a penultimate moving ultimately beyond itself?

It means that the quest for truth is ultimately penultimate. In the quest, reality is experienced as the mysterious movement of an It-reality through thing-reality toward a Beyond of things. Neither the things nor the non-things involved in this process are objects external to it; they are structures in the process, discerned through the quest for truth. Moreover, as the things and non-things are not external to the quest, the quest and its language are not external to them; in reflective distance, the quest itself is discerned as a "placed" event in the mysterious movement. For the questioner has to tell the story of his struggle for the unflawed order from his position in the flawed order of thingly existence; and he can tell it, therefore, only in the flawed language that speaks of non-things in the mode of things.

This flawed language includes the language of the "gods." Hence, the story of the quest does not put an End to the mystery but can only deepen the insight into its paradoxic penultimacy. Plato was acutely aware of this problem and expressed his awareness by distinguishing between the demiurgic act and the condition of thingness imposed upon it. With an ambiguity reminiscent of Hesiod, Plato lets the "being" of the triad Being-Becoming-Space precede in status the genesis of even the Ouranos (52D). The Demiurge, thus, is neither one of the things in Space like the "gods" who are created by him, nor is he a non-thing like the Cosmos that has Space, nor a non-thing like the non-thingly triad of Being-Becoming-Space that precedes the creation of even the "heaven," but a something whose only relation to Space is his submission to the "necessity" of creating "things" when creatively devising at all (47E–48A). This Demiurge, the radical non-thing beyond all thingness, properly resists determination in terms of thing-reality. "To find the Maker and Father of this *to pan* would be a job indeed; and even if found, to tell of him to all men would be impossible" (28C).

Although the movement of the quest beyond its "place" and its thingly language forces on Plato the same piling of beyond on beyond as is forced on Hesiod, however, in the philosopher's quest the movement becomes thematic. When the paradoxic experience of not-experientiable reality becomes conscious in reflective distance, the questioner's language reveals itself as the paradoxic event of the ineffable becoming effable. This tension of effable-ineffable is the paradox in the structure of meditative language that cannot be dissolved by a speculative meta-language of the kind by which Hegel wanted to dissolve the paradoxic "identity of identity and non-identity." In reflective distance, the questioner rather experiences his speech as the divine silence breaking creatively forth in the imaginative word that will illuminate the quest as the questioner's movement of return to the ineffable silence. The quest, thus, has no external "object" but is reality itself becoming luminous for its movement from the ineffable, through the Cosmos, to the ineffable. Moreover, the tensional structure of the movement will not allow either pole of the tension Demiurge-Necessity to become an "object." "The divine" (*to theion*) is no more an external object than "the necessary" (*to anagkaion*). Plato carefully stresses that "the divine" cannot be discerned by itself alone; there is no participation in "the divine" but through the exploration of the "things" in which it is discerned as formatively present (69A). The penultimate mystery of a Cosmos that exists in the tension of Taxis-Ataxia, in the tension of thing-reality and It-reality, becomes luminous for the ultimate mystery of a Creator-God who, when he creates, has to create a tensional Cosmos.

The study of the meditative process surrounding the symbol "Space" has been carried far enough to make it clear that the quest has indeed no "object" but is an event in tensional reality that raises the experienced tensions into consciousness. The language symbols emerging from the diversified tensions illuminate one another as well as the oneness of the quest in its wandering through the diversifications. In concluding these remarks, I cannot suppress the wish to see Plato's smile, if he could observe the contemporary spectacle of a "conquest of Space" after the spherical finiteness of the earth has let the ecumenic imperialists run out of space to be conquered.

12. [Untitled]

The experienced tensional constants and their symbolizations illuminate, complement, and balance one another in the quest for truth, but the questing wandering through the tensions does not arrive at an ultimate place of rest. None of the single tensions, or any of their poles, is an absolute entity given to an external observer; nor will the existentially balancing quest come to a rest in itself, but will remain a tensional event in a tensional Cosmos. The quest of which the tensions are an intelligible part is a movement within the thingly order of the Cosmos toward a Beyond of its thinglyness. Still, the meditative wandering through the penultimate tensions appears to become luminous for its Beginning in the ultimate mystery of a Creator-God who, when he creates, creates a tensional Cosmos. Is the Demiurge, then, the Absolute in which the tensional questioning comes to its End? We have to pursue this problem of the Absolute a few steps further, in order to gain a clear impression of Plato's empirical radicalism in the analysis of tensional experiences and their symbolization and of the consequences of this radicalism for understanding the language of the gods.

The Demiurge is not an Absolute either. His poietic action is experienced and symbolized as a complex of tensions between formative, noetic order and nonformative Space, between a demiurgic will to create order and the "necessary" obstacle of *chora* that limits the creative will to thingness. If then the divine Beginning is itself a complex of tensions, would perhaps the poles of the tensional complex at last be the Absolutes of reality? would the experienced Oneness of reality have to give way to some sort of "dualism"?

Plato avoids such a construction by symbolizing the poles of the tension themselves as tensional in character: (a) The Space at the lower pole of the complex is not a matter recognizable as such by its structure of a material element but a tensional something, symbolized metaphorically as a receptacle, or mother, or nurse of the visibly formed Cosmos, as an invisible, formless, all-receptive "kind of being." Because of its all-receptiveness for the persuasion of noetic order it is to be imagined as "partaking" of noetic order (*tou noetou*) "in an incomprehensible manner" (50B–51C). The thing-pole of the ultimate mystery, thus, is not itself a "thing" but a tensional kind of being, responsive to noetic order but imposing the mode of thingness on the Cosmos. The analysis seems to oppose something like a "thingly Beyond" at the lower pole of the demiurgic mystery to the "noetic Beyond" at its upper pole. (b) No less tensional in character is the divinely formative upper pole of the mystery. A *poietes* god, a Demiurge, devises and builds a tensional Cosmos from a Being that is never genesis and a Becoming that is never being. Confronted with this paradigmatic composition, one might well ask the question why the Demiurge did not leave the Always Being (*to on aei*) in its eternal existence, where it was free of tensions, rather than force it into the role of an ordering form for a Becoming in the mode of thingness? Does this creative and formative drive at the upper pole of the tensional complex not mean that the Demiurge, and the Being, partake "in an incomprehensible manner" of the *chora*, corresponding to the manner in which the *chora*, through its receptiveness, partakes incomprehensibly of the Nous? Does the noetic reality, symbolized as a "Beyond" of the tension, not desire to go "beyond" itself into the tension, just as the reality of Space, symbolized as a "Beyond" of material thingness, is ready to go "beyond" itself into thingly formed tensional reality?

But if the two poles of the mysterious tension each "partake" in correlative tensionality of the reality of the other pole, would then the "partaking" reality of the poles not be the one, true, mysterious reality rather than the tension symbolized by the poles? Plato appears to concede some sense to this possibility. For he considers it "proper to liken" the formative source, the "Wherefrom" (*to othen*) of Becoming to the Father of reality, and the recipient "Wherein" (*to d'en ho gignetai; to dechomenom*) of Becoming to its Mother, so that the tensional reality suspended between (*metaxy*) them would have to be conceived as their Offspring (*to ekgonos*) (50B–D). The metaphor of Father-Mother-Offspring, with its Pythagorean overtones, would seem to become the symbolism most suitably expressing the incomprehensible mystery of creative fertility in reality.

Any expectations of an ultimate symbolism, however, will again be disappointed. For the Offspring engendered in the metaxy of the Wherefrom and the Wherein is neither a physical equilibrium between two forces, nor a biological entity of unexplained further productivity, nor a consciousness in paralyzing suspense between two motivations, but cosmic reality "alive" in its tension of Taxis-Ataxia. Man, as part of the Offspring, experiences himself in a state, not of terminal paralysis, but of existential movement, responsively inclined to the pull from either of the two poles. Moreover, the pulls and inclinations are cognitively luminous for their meaning as movements beyond tensional existence toward nontensional reality in either the "thingly Beyond" of the *chora* or the "divine Beyond" of the *nous*. The movements, then, are not indifferently equal but distinguished in their meaning as (a) a movement toward a state of existence from which "as it were, God is absent" (53B) or (b) an immortalizing movement toward likeness (*homoiosis*) with God. In this complex of tensions experienced in the quest for truth as an event in cosmic reality, the "gods" play the equivocal role of a divine Beyond that demiurgically moves beyond itself into the formation of the Cosmos and, then, moves beyond its formative presence in the Cosmos toward its non-cosmic Beyond. Is the demiurgic Beyond that moves into the formation of a tensional Cosmos the same as the Beyond that saves from its tension? Is the god of the Beginning the same as the God of the End? The mystery of the demiurgic god, thus, is not ultimate but experienced as in tension toward the mystery of a divine reality that saves from the disorder of the Cosmos. The *fides* of the Cosmos becomes transparent for a drama of the Beyond enacted, through the tensional process of the Cosmos, from a demiurgic Beginning to a salvational End. No "Principles," or "absolutes," or "doctrines" can be extracted from this tensional complex; the quest for truth, as an event of participation in the process, can do no more than explore the structures in the divine mystery of the complex reality and, through the analysis of the experienced responses to the tensional pulls, arrive at some clarity about its own function in the drama in which it participates.

[12.*

The comprehending It-reality moves formatively through the thing-reality from a Beginning that does not begin in things to an End that does not end in things. The Beginning and the End of the story are experienced as a Beyond of the formative, tensional process of reality. There is no epiphany of structure in reality without a structuring force beyond the manifest structure; there is no revelation of divine ordering force in the quest for truth without a divine reality beyond the manifestation of its order in the event. The meditative wandering through the constants in the tensional process thus becomes luminous for a reality beyond the tensions that cannot be attained within tensional existence. The super-constant above

*Voegelin deliberately and carefully destroyed all draft pages of Volume V as he finished with them. The only exception was the following paragraph found on his desk. This page, numbered the same as the last section completed, was saved, probably because he hoped to work some of its thought and language into the meditation left unfinished.

the constants is not a principle of order whose proper application will dissolve the disorder of Cosmic order, but the experience of the paradoxic tension in formative reality, of the tension between the divine reality experienced as formatively present at the ordering pole of the tensions and the divine reality experienced as a Beyond of its concrete manifestations in the process, between the God who reveals himself in his presence in time and the God who remains the experienced but unknown reality beyond time. Moreover, the paradoxic tension in the revelation of formative reality is experienced as ultimate in the sense that intelligibly it cannot be out-experienced or out-symbolized by further experiences of reality. This experienced ultimacy of the tension becomes luminous in the symbol "divine."]

Epilogue

I

At the end of his introduction to the fourth volume of *Order and History*, *The Ecumenic Age*, the author announced that the fifth volume would be entitled *In Search of Order*. It was envisioned as a study of "the contemporary problems which have motivated the search for order in history."[1] But Eric Voegelin was not granted the time to complete this volume. The two chapters published here, as well as certain preliminary studies, published and unpublished, document the direction of his reflective analysis. But we do not know where the meditative search for order put into writing would have come to rest. And Voegelin would not have wanted us to know, because for him the end of the text is not determined by its beginning: "Although I have a general idea of its construction, I know from experience that new ideas have a habit of emerging while the writing is going on, compelling changes in the construction and making the beginning unsuitable."[2] Thus this final volume of *Order and History* remains the unfinished story of the author's search for order.

Yet the unfinished story of *Order and History* acquires an end, or *telos*, in itself at the very moment of being read by other men and women. It becomes "an event in a vast social field of thought and language, of writing and reading about matters that the members of the field believe to be of concern for their existence in truth."[3]

1. Eric Voegelin, *Order and History*, 5 vols. (1956–1987; available Columbia: University of Missouri Press, 1999), 4:58.
2. Ibid., 5:13; herein, 27.
3. Ibid.

The present volume, albeit brief, may then be experienced as a whole when it attains "a function in a communion of existential concern."[4] The end of the yet unfinished story is its existential effect on the minds and the hearts of people. And this efficacy of the story proves the truth of the tale of the search for order, told by the philosopher as distinguished from the many other storytellers of the time, giving his or her "private opinion concerning the order of his preference." The truth of the story is not warranted by the social or political standing of the person who tells the story. To the contrary, only a story that forces the listener by its truth to reorder his existence will turn out to be a true story of a philosopher's search for truth: "If the story is to evoke authoritatively the order of a social field, the word must be spoken with an authority recognizable as such by the men to whom the appeal is addressed; the appeal will have no authority of truth unless it speaks with an authority commonly present in everybody's consciousness, however inarticulate, deformed, or suppressed the consciousness in the concrete case may be."[5]

In this final volume of *Order and History* Voegelin restates the *telos,* or end, of his "inquiry in the classical sense of a *zetema,* a search for truth both cognitive and existential,"[6] that forms the whole of his philosophical inquiry into order and history. It has been conducted as a "search for truth concerning the order of being."[7] From the very beginning Voegelin was outspoken about the diagnostic and therapeutic functions of a philosophical inquiry. He intended to call forth islands of order amid the disorder of the age, thus reminding us of Kant's famous "island of truth surrounded by the wild and stormy ocean, the actual abode of delusion." The symbolism of the philosophical inquiry in itself may become the nucleus of some communion of existential concern in terms of a social field of existential order. Once people have formed social configurations grounded in common experiences of order, they enter the historical field delineated by man's search for his humanity and its order. If the story of man's search for truth is to be believed,

4. Ibid., 14; herein, 28.
5. Ibid., 26; herein, 40.
6. Eric Voegelin, "Toynbee's History as a Search for Truth," in *The Intent of Toynbee's History,* ed. Edward T. Gargan (Chicago: Loyola University Press, 1961), 183.
7. Eric Voegelin, *Israel and Revolution,* vol. I of *Order and History,* xiv.

then the existential concerns must be communicable so that the listener may share the philosopher's existential quest.

If the meaning of the philosopher's experience, meditation, and exegetic analysis are successfully conveyed to us, we readers mark the beginning of another story of the quest. Thus the story goes on, is taken up by other questioners, is continued as an act of open participation in the process of both history and the encompassing reality of the whole. The concerned listener makes it his own story and, for his part, begins another unfinished story. But the story of the philosophers does not begin with this particular person either. Voegelin's "word of the philosopher" has been structured by a millennial history of the philosophers' quest for truth, a history that has not stopped at some point in the past but is continuing in the present effort between reader and writer. "The social field constituted by the philosophers' language, thus, is not limited to communication through the spoken and written word among contemporaries, but extends historically from a distant past, through the present, into the future."[8] The philosophers' story, then, is the constant symbolic form of the ongoing quest for the order of existence.

The present historical situation, however, is pregnant with new philosophical developments; it calls for imaginative efforts toward a new symbolic mode of the questioner's search. This grand experiment of resymbolizing the experiences of reality motivated Voegelin's scholarship from his philosophical beginnings to the end of his life: To him *philosophy* meant "the creation of an order of symbols through which man's position in the world is understood."[9] The creation of such a symbolic form is the ultimate topic of this final volume of *Order and History*. Voegelin's true stature as a contemporary thinker emerges from these concluding pages more clearly than from most of his other writings. His philosophical inquiry unfolds in the historical context of the great symbolic enterprise of restating man's humanity under the horizon of the modern sciences and in resistance to the manifold forces of our age that deform human existence.

Voegelin was consistently engaged in a critical discourse with the great thinkers who struggled with the enormous task of making

8. Voegelin, *Order and History*, 5:14; herein, 28.
9. Eric Voegelin, *Anamnesis* (Munich: Piper, 1966), 59.

modern man understand himself. In this respect he must be seen on a line with Hegel, Schelling, Nietzsche, Heidegger, William James, and Whitehead, all of whom strove for the rediscovery of the experiential source of symbolization and identified the fundamental problems in the structure of consciousness, as Voegelin says when speaking of the irreversible intellectual achievements of Hegel. Voegelin, however, confronts the modern world more directly inasmuch as he makes the empirical knowledge being brought forth by the modern historical sciences the basis of any reflective analysis of reality. This empirical reality is discovered to be the experiential basis of the inquiring consciousness itself. Philosophical inquiry is conducted, not from the point of view of an outside observer, but by a participant observer who makes reality articulate. Thus Voegelin came to describe the inquiry as a mode of questioning, the responses being more or less differentiated insights into man's position in the whole of reality. If the inquirer is truly reality-bound, his scientific exploration of the phenomena that delineate the realm of man advances not only cognitive but also existential truth. Advance in existential truth means a more differentiated explication of the paradoxical structure of human existence in the tension between earthly existence and the formative ground of all being within an encompassing prepersonal reality that in itself remains an ultimate mystery. The methodological postulate of cognitive openness toward the whole range of experience is intertwined with the existential postulate of the meditative openness toward the source of ordering experience. Such openness denotes reason as the constituent of man's humanity as it was discovered in the epochal event of Hellenic philosophy.

II

The original program of *Order and History* called for a philosophical inquiry into man's advance from the truth of cosmic-divine order to the differentiated experience of transcendent-divine order in Israel and Hellas. Unlike the break with the cosmological order and the world of the myth in China and India, these Western modes of the differentiated consciousness and their attendant symbolic forms, Revelation and Philosophy, gave conscious *historical form* to the order of human existence in society. Therefore, the philosopher's discovery in retrospect of the history of mankind presupposes the symbolic explication of the historicity of human existence in the West, the philosophy of order and history being exclusively a Western symbolism. Without Revelation, Voegelin argued, there would be no problem of the history of mankind; and without Philosophy, the history of mankind would not be a problem of philosophy. From the authoritative communications about the truth of being in the Western historical form emerges the Logos of history itself. In other words, the language of these authoritative communications about the truth of being provides also the language of the modern analyst's study concerning the order of existence in society and history. The terms of the philosophical inquiry evolve from the critical understanding of the historically differentiated experiences and their symbolizations; they are, however, still tied to the symbolic tradition bequeathed to us by the Greeks, the Jews, and the Christians. The dynamics of the ensuing empirical research propelled the philosophical reflection toward new horizons. The critical turn in Voegelin's thought involved the need for a "more differentiated language than that of classical philosophy."[10]

The fourth volume, *The Ecumenic Age*, reinforces the critical turn in Voegelin's view of the contemporary philosopher's responsibility for critical language that is to reconstruct from the symbolic materials of the past the quest for order in the present and to re-create the philosopher's language in responding to the quest. This office implied "the return from symbols which have lost their meaning to the experiences which constitute meaning" by dismantling "the massive block of accumulated symbols, secondary and tertiary," which are the great obstacle to this return.[11] In *The Ecumenic Age*, therefore, Voegelin reformulates the conception of the philosophical inquiry in terms of the *Question* understood as the underlying constant of the historical manifold of human self-actualization. From the plurality of answers springs the plurality of types of order and their symbolic forms, which in their entirety reflect the comprehending reality of *universal humanity*. These reflections, Voegelin explains, "are the mode of questioning engendered in the contemporary situation by a philosopher's resistance to the distortion and destruction of humanity committed by the 'stop-history' Systems."[12]

10. Ibid., 347.
11. Voegelin, *Order and History*, 4:58.
12. Ibid., 335.

The study of order and history is thus a questioning, an open-ended quest for truth. It will never result in an ultimate answer or an absolute truth, an absolute order, permanent values, propositions, principles, ideals, or doctrines. Consequently, the symbols developed in the course of reflective analysis have to be carefully guarded against libidinous misuse by the power brokers of the time. The philosopher's language must not be of service to the lust for power among spiritual and other imperialists. Voegelin's reflective efforts at symbolization disclose a growing penchant for de-doctrinalization. The recovery of the experiences of reality implies the emancipation from deformed language that is dissociated from the engendering experiences.

In *The Ecumenic Age* Voegelin had pursued this problem to the point at which the language of the questioning itself became the subject of reflection. This shift in the focus of analysis prompted Voegelin to deliberate once more the historical attainment of the Hellenic philosophers. The questioning philosopher revisits his antecedents in that their symbolization of man's search for his humanity and its order articulated for the first time in history the structure of the quest itself, resulting in the epochal formative achievement of *reason*, the key symbol designating the "cognitively luminous center of order in existence."[13]

The philosopher's reason represents the specific humanity of man as that of a "questioner for the wherefrom and the whereto, for the ground and the sense of his existence. Though this questioning is inherent to man's experience of himself at all times, the adequate articulation and symbolization of the questioning consciousness as the constituent of humanity is . . . the epochal feat of the philosophers."[14] In effect, this epochal feat of the philosophers culminates in Plato's work with the discovery of the quest itself as a source of order and disorder in existence, with the exploration of its structure, and with the creation of a language that will express the discovery.[15] This language of truth becoming luminous in the questioning consciousness enables the philosopher to understand and interpret the rich historical field of symbolizations

13. Eric Voegelin, "Reason: The Classic Experience," *Southern Review* n.s. 10 (1974): 240, in *CW*, 12:265–91, at 268.
14. Ibid., 241, in *CW*, 12:268–69.
15. Eric Voegelin, "Wisdom and the Magic of the Extreme: A Meditation," *Southern Review* n.s. 17 (1981): 235–87, in *CW*, 12:315–75.

manifesting man's search for his humanity and its order, uncovering truth and untruth of the manifold different tongues of the human quest. Turning "reflectively toward the area of reality called human existence"[16] is to critically study the equivalent field of experiences and symbolizations that signifies the images of truth evolving in history from the anonymous process of reality. Accepting the symbols as self-expressive manifestations of a truth, the reflective inquiry into their meaning will make them more intelligible as a component of the symbolic whole that is universal humanity. This privileged position of the philosopher presupposes the philosopher's will and capacity to reactivate the engendering experience in his psyche and to recapture the truth of reality living in the symbols by means of his own meditative efforts. Voegelin, thus, places a new emphasis on the philosopher's role as an existentially participant observer and on the language of his inquiry. From his remembering knowledge springs, by the power of his imagination, the philosopher's own image of reality in terms of symbolization that he recognizes as part of the historical field and that is constituted by the equivalent modes of experience and symbolization. Noetic reflection evokes this historical field from the accumulated materials of empirical knowledge.

III

In "The Beginning and the Beyond," an earlier study [published in *CW*, 28:173–232], Voegelin came right to the key question: What is the inquiry itself?—the question forced upon the thinker by the present situation in which there is no accepted language or literary form for dealing with the fundamental problems of truth and language raised by the present state of empirical knowledge concerning the "historical manifold" of social reality.[17] This question extends to the use of the symbols of the past as analytical concepts in our time. "Their critical value as instruments of interpretation must be re-examined and since this re-examination extends to our common language of 'philosophy,' 'being,' 'theology,' 'religion,' 'myth,' 'reason,''revelation,' and so forth, a considerable upheaval in the conventional use of these symbols is to

16. Eric Voegelin, "Equivalences of Experience and Symbolization in History," *Philosophical Studies* 28 (1981): 89, in *CW*, 12:115–33, at 116.
17. Voegelin, "The Beginning and the Beyond," 188.

be expected."[18] But the creation of an "entirely new universe of symbols" is not envisioned, since the ongoing conceptual work of reflection can retrieve the original language of experiential analysis from its doctrinal deformation and reassert its meaning in the present quest. These reflections on the legitimacy of the methods of the inquiry and the criteria of its truth elucidate the crucial problem of the "hermeneutic experience" (Gadamer)—i.e., the genuine understanding of the truth of language-symbols transmitted to us from the past. Reflective inquiry into the meaning of the historical language symbols, Voegelin suggests, could and should make more intelligible the truth put forth by those symbols. He states very clearly the assumption underlying his position: The meaning of the symbols can be detached from the original language in order to translate it critically into the language of reflective analysis, a hermeneutic procedure that assumes that "the original symbols . . . contain, however compactly veiled, a rational structure that can be made intelligible through reflection."[19]

These remarks on the hermeneutics of the reflective study of symbols spell out the fundamental requirement of Voegelin's theory of consciousness: "a comprehensive philosophy concerning the truth of reality"[20] in which both the original symbols as well as the reflective symbols, neither set being external objects of cognition whose truth can be judged by external criteria, break forth from the common reality that is the constant underlying all equivalents of experience and symbolization. Thus, the articulation of the rational structure contained in the historical modes of symbolization by means of reflective analysis reveals a process of reality becoming cognitively luminous in the human enterprise of the questioning search. The philosopher, like every man in search of his humanity, participates consciously in the existential drama of the Platonic In-Between of mortality and immortality. But the philosopher's reflective acts of cognition—as Voegelin states in volume V, referring once more to the first philosopher Plato—are distinguished by the precarious balance they strike between the finality of the language of truth experienced and articulated historically and the

18. Ibid., 230.
19. Ibid., 189.
20. Eric Voegelin, "Outline: Structure of Consciousness," 2, unpublished manuscript, now in Hoover Institution Library, Stanford University.

nonfinality determined by the language's position in an ongoing, open-ended process.

This balance of noetic or reflective consciousness is the specific differentiating attainment of philosophizing insofar as it articulates the dimension of reflective distance in consciousness. By introducing the term "reflective distance" Voegelin designates the reflective acts of consciousness and the concomitant reflective symbolization as the authentic area of the philosophical inquiry. Reflective distance bridges the gap between the "absolute" truth experienced by a person and the "relative" truth documenting itself in the historical manifold of human self-expression. Reflective distance brings out the interplay between the philosopher's imaginative attempts at symbolization and the remembering activity of his consciousness that is noetic anamnesis. The language of reflective distance refers analytically to the personal dimension of human existence in terms of the meditative complex of consciousness-reality-language that provides the symbols with their contextual validity; it relates to the social dimension of human existence in terms of a social field of public consciousness, which furnishes the mutual understanding of existentially committed human beings. And, finally, it is concerned with the historical dimension of human existence in terms of man's search for his humanity and its order that assigns to the symbols their validity in the context of their historical equivalences. From this critical analysis of the philosophical inquiry comes forth the reflective language framing the symbolic form of modern man's questioning, which is the subject matter of the present volume.

Voegelin's analysis of the reflective dimension of consciousness is informed by Hegel's attempt at recovering the experiential roots of consciousness. In opposition to, and as corrective of, the symbolism of reflective identity, Voegelin says, he has formulated the symbolism of reflective distance. Following the lead of Hegel's self-analysis in the *Phaenomenologie des Geistes*, Voegelin reenacts by means of anamnesis the true story of the unfolding reflective consciousness from its mythopoetic origins in Hesiod to its full differentiation in Plato-Socrates. In the course of his penetrating reinterpretation of Platonic philosophy Voegelin lays out his own exegesis of the questioning consciousness. The process of questioning unravels with great analytical care the structural whole of reality consciously experienced as the meaningful epiphany of material, animal, and human being in reality.

While the epiphany of structure in reality itself remains "a mystery inaccessible to explanation"[21] (science being engaged in a never-ending uncovering of one structural determinant after another), the meditative movement of questioning gravitates toward the structuring force beyond manifest structure. The quest is experienced as the irruption of ordering force from an intangible and ineffable Beyond into the existential struggle for order in the common human world. This experience of a fundamental tension in existential reality pointing toward an order beyond itself is ultimate: "This experienced ultimacy of the tension becomes luminous in the symbol 'divine.' "[22]

In Search of Order was conceived as the philosopher's finishing touch to the conceptual work of reflection. The final and radical recasting of the reflective symbolization of man's quest of his humanity under the horizon of the modern world remains unfinished. But the contours of a philosophy of the human condition are vividly extant in *In Search of Order.*

Energetically and relentlessly pressing for a de-doctrinalized language of reflective analysis, Voegelin's grand design for reflective symbolization falls within the scope of the varied modes of philosophical language analysis from Humboldt and Charles S. Peirce to Wittgenstein, which also was conducted as a critique of the dogmatic traditions. Voegelin shares the intention to reflect upon the linguistic propositions of philosophy itself and the attendant problems of the scientific languages. He also partakes of the insight that the philosopher's specific language is reflectively and critically related to all possible languages.

But Voegelin resolves cogently the fundamental *aporia* of a strictly formalistic and instrumentalistic approach to language that is forced to posit a transcendental ideal community of communication void of any empirical content. Bypassing any transcendental constructions Voegelin traces the reflective language back to reflective consciousness, articulating the Logos of reality that all human beings partake of. This partnership in being, as revealed in man's quest for his humanity, is the precondition of the possibility

---

21. Voegelin, *Order and History,* 5:17; herein, 31.
22. Ibid., 107; herein, 124 *ad fin.*.

of language per se. The cultivation of this existential knowledge having an eminent bearing on the social order is the philosopher's responsibility in any time of crisis. Voegelin therefore followed this call to the philosopher's duty in his imaginative response to the modern challenge to human reason. His quest for truth was carried on with the determination to restore the common logos of meditative reality to the state of public consciousness in a time of cognitive and existential dissonance.

JÜRGEN GEBHARDT

Index